So many times what Tracy wrote struck a personal chord with me! I loved the stories she chose to share and the messages she pulled from them. Tracy has a wonderful gift for painting vivid pictures based on biblical stories with modern-day parallels and even describing what our heavenly reunion might be like. She really drew me in.

—Kathy Ide, author, editor, and owner of
Christian Editor Network

I like the topics Tracy chose to write about; several of them spoke to me and piqued my interest. She has a lot to offer readers. I found inspiration in the material I read.

—Lori Shire, Ashland Theological Seminary, Master of arts in
Biblical studies for both Old and New Testament

This book is a life-saving manual meant for any soul who has bottomed out and can only look up for help.

—George Firehammer, lay leader
Spotsylvania, Virginia

Tracy's use of biblical stories and relating them to our everyday lives is spot on.

—Betsy Johnson, member of Nomads on Missions (NOMADS)

A model for those who seek a stronger faith. The content is beautifully written and will help a lot of folks.

—Libby Wharton, active Stephen Minister for 19 years

Refuge OF GRACE

finding your safe place

TRACY L. SMOAK

Bold Vision Books
PO Box 2011
Friendswood, TX 77549

ISBN 978-1-946708-95-3
Library of Congress Number 2023945552
All rights reserved.
Published by Bold Vision Books, PO Box 2011, Friendswood, Texas 77549
www.boldvisionbooks.com

Cover Design by Barefaced Creative Media - Amber Wiegand-Buckley
Interior design by WendyEL Creative
Published in the United States of America.
Edited by kae Creative Solutions

Scripture quotations marked (NIV) are taken from the Holy Bible, New International Version®, NIV®. Copyright © 1973, 1978, 1984, 2011 by Biblica, Inc.™ Used by permission of Zondervan. All rights reserved worldwide. www.zondervan.com The "NIV" and "New International Version" are trademarks registered in the United States Patent and Trademark Office by Biblica, Inc.™

May God's word equip generations
to live victoriously
and bring Him glory

May God's
love
secure
you.
Tracy

CONTENTS

FOREWORD

The Lord provides people to break open the Bread of Life, God's written Word, to feed our weary souls. Tracy Smoak is among the people He is using. The need is now; this book is timely; her source is timeless. When our hearts are downcast, Tracy's word pictures come alongside, meeting the reader where she or he is. But her words do not leave the reader there. Rather, they point the way forward to the deep well of reviving water to be found in Scripture. Her words do not just stand as a road sign pointing us in the direction of the Word. Somehow her writing accompanies us from our hard places to God's healing promises.

As Tracy's former pastor, I hear beneath the sentences, bubbling up through the words, the challenges, losses, grief, disappointments, and broken relationships she has experienced. When she identifies specific situations that grind down or radically undermine our hope, you can be sure she is speaking from her life story. She has lived a life that has needed a renewal of hope time and again. And God has delivered it for her. Now she shares that encouragement with you through *Refuge of Grace: Finding Your Safe Place.*

—Rev. Dr. Stephen Hay, retired

Chapter One

NO WEAPON FORGED AGAINST YOU WILL PREVAIL

*I*s everything topsy-turvy in your life?

Maybe what you once could count on has collapsed. You're trying to get your bearings and tiptoeing to find solid footing again. You question what's safe in the slippery mud of uncertainty, and your faith may falter a bit.

If so, let this book remind you God's promises are true and his presence in your life is steadfast. His love will help you navigate the unknowns, just as he has guided others for millennia. Journey anew through Bible stories to see ways God can speak to you during trials and help you overcome every difficulty. With him, you are secure.

You know this, but you might feel weary and discouraged. You have withstood onslaught after onslaught and don't feel as though you can muster strength to repel another attack.

Take heart, beloved. "No weapon forged against you will prevail" (Isaiah 54:17). God sees your trial and will secure you. His timing may not be what you want, nor may his deliverance be quite what you expect, but his victory in your life is certain.

When chaos capsizes you, and you flail about for solid footing, look for Christ's banner. Turn your eyes toward the golden flag embroidered with a scarlet cross. Listen for the trumpet's call rallying the troops. Take up your position. Stand firm. He who is faithful races to your rescue.

Look at the horizon and keep watch for the Rider named Faithful and True (Revelation 19:11). He's mounted on a white war stallion with mane flowing, nostrils flaring, and hooves thundering on the turf. Jesus is this divine warrior leaning forward in the saddle. He, whose love for you is hot as erupting lava, charges forward to bring justice and wage war against those who oppose truth. "His eyes are like blazing fire, and on his head are many crowns" (Revelation 19:12).

His holy presence inspires hope because he fights on your behalf with all of God's assets at his command. Right behind Jesus march the armies of heaven, and these stalwart soldiers are dressed in fine linen and riding on alabaster horses (Revelation 19:14).

Hold on just a little longer. You can do it. Muster faith to see forward.

Yet you wonder, *How am I supposed to do that?*

You are face-planted on the ground, mud caked on your face, and your shield dented. You dropped your sword some distance away. The enemy has worn you down. You're not sure you can get back up, much less stand. Images of you as a valiant soldier collapse. Truth be told, tears of frustration and sorrow streak down the grime on your cheek. You taste salty disappointment. Real warriors don't cry, or do they?

Rest where you are for a moment. What needs to be done will be achieved with God's strength, not yours. If you need time to collect yourself, that's OK. God takes pride in his children who are overcomers. He sees the pain. He knows the desperation. Yet when one of his loved ones stands on shaky legs to arise again, it brings him great pleasure. Angels sing "hallelujah" and cymbals clang when the weary trust.

The Bible is full of stories of frail people who achieved the impossible, not because they were perfect, but because in weakness, they chose to rely on God. Consider this paradox from Ezekiel. God instructs the prophet to foretell a mighty army will be gathered from many nations to attack Israel. Enemy troops would advance "like a storm" (Ezekiel 38:9) to attack peaceful and unsuspecting people.

What stalks you? Is it a financial shortfall? Or health issues? Maybe family rifts tear the fabric of your identity and security. You might feel helpless against the evil intent to plunder and loot your peace of mind. A great horde advances upon you. You fend off one adversity, only to see two more problems coming straight at you with sharpened lances pointed at your heart. Sometimes, even believers shake in their boots and let their hands hang useless in terror.

Just when you want to give up and flee the scene, you notice confusion in the enemy ranks. When you didn't have a chance, God intervenes. He will strike the bows from the attackers' left hand and make their arrows drop harmlessly (Ezekiel 39:3).

God defeats the enemy right in front of you. "I will make known my holy name among my people Israel. I will no longer let my holy name be profaned, and the nations will know that I the Lord am the Holy One in Israel" (Ezekiel 39:7).

With God's presence, your fears now seem silly as the imminent doom transforms into a prosperous boon. Every danger you face can be the spark further igniting your faith. The Israelites in this prophecy enjoy God's protection and later take all the enemy's gear and re-purpose the spoils. "Then those who live in the towns of Israel will go out and use the weapons for fuel and burn them up—the small and large shields, the bows, and arrows, the war clubs and spears" (Ezekiel 39:9).

Whether trials originate in temptations or in being targeted, God can use these experiences to strengthen and enrich you. God converts what the enemy intends for destruction into a wealth of resources. Consider how much work went into finding firewood in ancient times. There was no easy flick of a switch. To survive and cook food, people labored to gather fuel. Now, instead of struggling, the Israelites found abundance at their fingertips. As the chosen ones collected the enemy spears littering the land, they realized how much God cared for their every need.

Have you taken time lately to remember how much God has blessed you? Even in a season of loss or struggle, there is much to celebrate. How ironic that what the enemy plans for devastation becomes a blessing.

Financial crisis? Hang in there. You may find God uses the shortage to teach you better management, then he entrusts you with even more money to invest in building his kingdom.

Got cancer or herniated discs? Perhaps pain garners compassion so you may comfort others.

Suffered the loss of a loved one? How does grief reveal the depth of God's desire for you in his eternal kingdom? He sacrificed everything so he could have you with him. Because Jesus defeated even death, separation isn't forever for those who are his children.

God's victory will be so great the enemy's gear may sustain you for years to come. "For seven years they (Israelites) will use them (war spoils) for fuel. They will not need to gather wood from the fields or cut it from the forests because they will use the weapons for fuel" (Ezekiel 39:9-10). Imagine the utility company sending you a letter saying your account is prepaid for seven years.

Even amid warfare, keep your focus on the One known as Faithful and True. He can redeem any failure and restore any broken dream. He is the healer. With confidence, go out to face the struggles. The Lord will be with you (2 Chronicles 20:17). He enjoys plot twists. Just as he turned the attackers' swords into toothpicks, so will he convert your problems into assets for advancing his righteous rule. He loves you.

God promises he will never leave you nor forsake you (Joshua 1:5).

FOR REFLECTION

*"No weapon forged against you will prevail, and you will refute
every tongue that accuses you. This is the heritage of the servants of
the Lord, and this is their vindication from me,"
declares the Lord (Isaiah 54:17).*

Life is a battle between the forces of good and evil. God will be victorious, and if you align yourself with him, you will be too. The idea of a weapon being forged means an enemy plans and attempts to damage you, but there are no secrets kept from the Lord. He sees the hardships you will encounter and will not let you be defeated.

What forces are against you now? Try creating a T-chart on a sheet of notebook paper. Label the left side "Weapons against me" and the right side "God's promises to stand on." Quietly examine both sides of the chart. At the end of each chapter, there is a promise from God to treasure.

For every difficulty you must overcome, God pledges to stand with you. Every hardship is an opportunity to build your faith so you can testify about hope to others.

A PRAYER FOR TODAY

*Dear Lord, I am tired and feel afraid. Circumstances threaten to
overwhelm me. Please strengthen my resolve to keep moving forward
in faith. Please carry me during the times I can't walk.
Lift my eyes to see your steadfast love. Amen*

Chapter Two

BE CAREFUL NOT TO FORGET THE LORD YOUR GOD

*G*od pulled you through a tough scene. You're ready to rest awhile. But don't get too comfortable. Landing in a cushy place has drawbacks. You might not feel you need God as much when pressure subsides. Wouldn't it be tempting to coast?

The urgency for Bible study isn't as strong. Prayer gets crowded out by other pressing activities. Seeking of the Lord dwindles. You can always talk with God later. After all, he is available 24/7.

However, take heed to what happened to the Israelites when they felt entitled. After 400 years of slavery in Egypt and their miraculous exodus, you'd think they would have God flashing on their minds like neon signs in Times Square. God supplied plenty of sweet water and manna for his children during 40 years of desert survival as he purified and strengthened them.

When the Israelites started getting restless and wanted more, Moses reminded them, "Your clothes did not wear out and your feet did not swell during these forty years" (Deuteronomy 8:4). Taking daily supplies for granted is easy, if you always have them.

Moses didn't want the Israelites to become prideful in their abundance. He said, "When you have eaten and are satisfied, praise the

Lord your God for the good land he has given you. Be careful that you do not forget the Lord your God, failing to observe his commands" (Deuteronomy 8:10-11).

With all their needs met by God, the Israelites might puff up in conceit. Moses warned: "Otherwise, when you eat and are satisfied, when you build fine houses and settle down, and when your herds and flocks grow large and your silver and gold increase and all you have is multiplied, then your heart will become proud and you will forget the Lord your God, who brought you out of Egypt, out of the land of slavery" (Deuteronomy 8:12-14).

Has pride sauntered up to tempt you? God's bountiful provision becomes a feat *you* accomplished. Hard work, brains, and ambition equipped you to have everything. After all, you earned that diploma and paycheck. Leaving God out of the equation is easy when you perch on the mountain and view the valley. Be careful not to topple off the heights.

Be sure to give God praise for the gifts he's bestowed. Moses counseled the Israelites: "He led you through the vast and dreadful wilderness, that thirsty and waterless land, with its venomous snakes and scorpions. He brought you water out of hard rock" (Deuteronomy 8:15). During every defining moment, God has stood right by and guided you. He has given you the natural talents and divine opportunities to succeed. Remember to give him credit. Let him know how much you appreciate his presence.

Sometimes, trials are pop quizzes to help you recall important truths. "He gave you manna to eat in the wilderness, something your ancestors had never known, to humble and test you so that in the end it might go well with you" (Deuteronomy 8:16). Arrogance takes God's abundance and calls into question when more is coming. This trap spoils the pleasure of gifts at your fingertips and tarnishes their enjoyment.

Pride leaves no room for God. You might be tempted to think, "My power and the strength of my hands have produced this wealth for me" (Deuteronomy 8:17). This conceit may be more deadly than an armed enemy charging at you. At least with an attacker, you see the danger for what it is. Pride creeps in by degrees until you are blinded by the cataract of self. If you are entranced gazing in the mirror, there's not much room to see God.

To counteract this, Moses advised, "But remember the Lord your God, for it is he who gives you the ability to produce wealth, and so confirms his covenant" (Deuteronomy 8:18). Enjoy the good times. Celebrate seeing dreams fulfilled. But never forget who gave you the vision or ability to accomplish goals.

One Bible hero who wrestled with pride was David. Studies often focus on his early heroic feats, such as felling the giant Goliath with a rock and slingshot. This young shepherd from humble beginnings became ruler over Judah in his 30s. From Hebron, David led for seven and a half years battling his treacherous former father-in-law, Saul (2 Samuel 5:4-5).

During this period, David acquired six wives (2 Samuel 3:2). He also required his first spouse, who was Saul's daughter Michal, be returned to him, even though she had remarried after David fled to escape being murdered by Saul.

Michal's second spouse, Paltiel, wept and followed the military unit taking her back to David until the soldiers turned him away (2 Samuel 3:13-15). Though social customs of the time encouraged political alliances through marriage, you wonder how much David's ego drove his decisions.

David's status grew while the house of Saul weakened. After Saul's death fighting Philistines, the elders of Israel approached David in Hebron to covenant with him as their leader (2 Samuel 5:1-3). With their support, David conquered Jerusalem, which he established as the City of David. Why didn't he call the new fortress the City of God? With David's newfound prestige, did he forget his Lord?

In Jerusalem, David "took more concubines and wives" (2 Samuel 5:13). He expanded his empire, as well as his sense of entitlement.

The trappings of success and privilege would trip him up, and the pride of his prime would become his nightmare.

David wasn't content with the gifts God showered upon him. David wanted more to serve his ego. He seduced the wife of his trusted soldier, Uriah, while Uriah was away fighting to bring David accolades. (2 Samuel 23:39) David's prideful desire for the lovely Bathsheba resulted in God's ire. (2 Samuel 11)

God corrected David through Nathan: "I anointed you king over Israel, and I delivered you from the hand of Saul. I gave your master's house to you, and your master's wives into your arms. I gave you all Israel and Judah. And if all this had been too little, I would have given you even more. Why did you despise the word of the Lord by doing what is evil in his eyes?" (2 Samuel 12:7-10).

The evil had grievous consequences. David's first six sons born in Hebron had six different mothers (2 Samuel 3:1-5). Family rivalries ruptured David's household. The firstborn son, Amnon, lusted for his half-sister Tamar and raped her (2 Samuel 13:1-22). David's third son, Absalom, who shared the same mother as Tamar, gave his disgraced sister refuge in his home. But all the while, he hated Amnon for the crime.

When David didn't exile Amnon, Absalom took matters in his own hands. With two years of plotting, Absalom arranged a party and executed Amnon in front of the other brothers (2 Samuel 13:23-29). Absalom then fled to his maternal grandfather's kingdom in Geshur for three years (2 Samuel 13:37).

Eventually, David allowed Absalom to return to Jerusalem. But the unfortunate legacy of pride poisoned the family again as Absalom spent four years seeking favor from the people. When Absalom recruited sufficient followers, he led a rebellion against his own father.

Contrary to David's orders, Israelite troops killed the traitorous Absalom. Despite being handsome, privileged, and popular, Absalom's ambition destroyed him.

Does pride endanger you? Reflect carefully on what motivates you. If you seek recognition and desire more power, kneel in prayer. Humble yourself before the Lord. Ask him to give you eyes to see your errors. If your heart is not right before God's throne, you cannot sustain victory in life's battles.

David suffered more setbacks because of the unhealthy self-centeredness he modeled. The pattern of royal revolt by another arrogant son would repeat. This would happen at the end of David's 40-year rule with his fourth son from Hebron.

When old age confined King David to his bed, his servants found a young virgin to lie beside him and keep him warm (1 Kings 1). The elderly David shivered in his cedar bed under a soft, purple quilt. He who created hundreds of songs and played the harp danced no more. Though known for his athleticism, his body now betrayed him with aches.

The scriptures don't tell what David thought, but you can't help wonder if he felt lonely and hoped for a visit from family or friends. The one who commanded armies and slayed tens of thousands was helpless to force love.

While David shakes under blankets, another conspiracy fueled by conceit grows. The next handsome and willful son, Adonijah, whose mother was Haggith, brazenly maneuvers to seize control. "I will be king" (1 Kings 1:6).

With these four short words, Adonijah abandons God. He places himself at the center of the universe and abandons any notion of service to the Holy One. Do you do the same? Do you place your agenda before God's?

Adonijah confers with David's general and priest, then throws a massive party to celebrate his coronation, without his father's blessing (1 Kings 1:1-5). Word gets out about the impending power transfer, and God has the faithful prophet, Nathan, interrupt festivities. David learns about Adonijah's scheme and declares his son Solomon by

Bathsheba as his successor instead. How sad David's final hours are marred by dissension and competition for his position as king.

Don't let pride goad you into selfish choices, which can wreck a family or community. "Pride brings a person low, but the lowly in spirit gain honor" (Proverbs 29:23).

Instead of elevating your own name, open your heart to the joy of being present with Jesus. Thank him for guiding and protecting you. Treasure God's loving kindness. Titles and fame are temporary. Nothing short of intimacy with God will fully satisfy.

> *God promises if you humble yourself, seek his face in prayer, and turn from wicked ways, he will hear from heaven and forgive your sin and heal the land (2 Chronicles 7:14).*

FOR REFLECTION

"Remember how the Lord your God led you all the way in the wilderness these forty years, to humble you and test you in order to know what was in your heart, whether or not you would keep his commands" (Deuteronomy 8:2).

Think about your interactions with God. Do you only go to him when you want something? Calibrate your expectations about prestige beyond what you might "get" from God. Are you aspiring to create your own kingdom at the expense of His?

Evaluate relationships you have. Are you always the giver or do you cash in on many favors? Consider how these can be balanced for healthier interactions. What simple, sentimental gift could you offer to your heavenly king today to bring him joy?

A PRAYER FOR TODAY

Dear Lord, Please protect me from pride. So often, I am tempted to take credit for your blessings to me. I get caught up wanting the limelight and forget to give you glory. Thank you very much for all the gifts you've given. My very ability to breathe is your life in me. Please help me see where you are at work today and join you in willing service with no expectation for reward or acclaim. Amen

Chapter Three

CALL TO GOD AND HE WILL ANSWER

*A*s any good lieutenant, you study the battlefield and await orders from the commander-in-chief. You acknowledge Jesus as the Righteous Ruler and understand he will be victorious. You submit to his authority. Yet in the skirmish ahead, you need help to discern the strategy how to take the ground assigned to you. How God's full campaign will unfold is unclear.

Moving forward in the dark with fog makes tense moments. You want to charge to your position, but the opaque curtain blocks your view of what's ahead. You are forced to slow down and creep along with little visibility. Eerie glows distort scenery with strange silhouettes. Given the conditions, you do not know how to proceed.

Jeremiah of the sixth century B.C. knew all about unsettling situations. As a young man, he began his ministry working for a righteous king who led efforts to bring the people of Judah into alignment with God's rules. This King Josiah purified the temples, got rid of false priests, and renewed the peoples' covenant with God (2 Kings 23:1-15).

The faithful turned back to God, and the community prospered. "Neither before nor after Josiah was there a king like him who turned to the Lord as he did—with all his heart and with all his soul and with all his strength, in accordance with all the Law of Moses" (2 Kings 23:25).

Maybe you have had a terrific boss or teacher who followed godly principles, and the workplace was orderly and productive. But then, management changed and all the hard-won progress started unraveling. Will you hold your position even when difficulties arise?

Jeremiah did. He held onto faith when King Josiah died battling the Egyptian Pharaoh Necho at Megiddo. After 31 years with a strong leader at the helm, the crown of Judah transferred to King Josiah's twenty-three-year-old son, Jehoahaz.

In short order, decades of stability crashed. Chaos ran rampant. Within three months, Pharaoh Necho captured Jehoahaz, put chains on him, and removed him from Jerusalem (2 Kings 23:33). The testing of Jeremiah's faith began.

Have you been in a situation where everything fell apart, and no one seemed to know how to fix the problem? One directive competes with the next. Collaboration collapses while petty kingdoms fight for supremacy. Uncertainty rules while onlookers assess which power broker will emerge victorious. God may direct you to serve there and model steadfastness.

Necho exacted a huge tax of gold and silver from the people of Judah. He also established a puppet regime with Jehoahaz's slightly older brother. This Jehoiakim controlled Jerusalem for 11 years and "did evil in the eyes of the Lord" (2 Chronicles 36:4-5). Jeremiah must have been terrified. His beloved king was gone, and the enemy controlled the new one. Yet Jeremiah kept marching forward and calling out to God for guidance.

What do you do when everything falls apart? Do you lie low and watch the fireworks from a safe distance? Do you give up and run away? Jeremiah wrote songs of grief for Josiah, but he didn't dissolve in his sorrow (2 Chronicles 35:25).

Jeremiah remained stalwart because he remembered what God commanded years ago at his commissioning as a prophet. "…You must go to everyone I send you to and say whatever I command you" (Jeremiah 1:7). Jeremiah lived out his faith, even when it wasn't easy.

God told Jeremiah not to worry about kings, officials, priests, or other people. He promised Jeremiah: "Do not be afraid of them, for I am with you and will rescue you" (Jeremiah 1:8).

Maybe you worry about what's the right thing to say, particularly when people deviate from God's commands. You want to choose the high road, but fear doing so might anger others. If you ask God, he will direct you how to lead in dark times.

God's favor often brings privileges, but not always. Not because God doesn't care or want to give you the best, but because others want to silence the truth he will speak. God wants you to correct wrongs and model obedience to him. This is what leaders do on the battlefield of life. Empowered by God, the faithful combat the enemy's schemes.

If others resist the holy principles you share with them in loving respect, know God will strengthen you to deliver the message he wants to go forth. Whether the conversations are with family, co-workers or in social gatherings, delivering words for positive change is not for the faint-hearted. But if believers don't step up, who will?

God told Jeremiah: "I have made you a fortified city, an iron pillar and a bronze wall to stand against the whole land ... They will fight against you but will not overcome you, for I am with you and will rescue you" (Jeremiah 1:18-19). When others stray, don't hit them over the head with religious mantras to knock sense into them. Serving as an agent for change requires delicate negotiation.

However, biting your tongue may not be what God wants either. You may be in a pivotal place, positioned by God, to call people back to him and remind them of his love with gentle words of truth. You may be the only spokesperson to help them correct the course of their life, and avoid defeat.

If a person's romantic relationship is generating temptation, is it kinder to offer concern or to let the person run headlong into disaster? Maybe bitterness is destroying the family. Coaching on the value of forgiveness, rather than pandering to hurt feelings, may be the honesty needed for true healing. In a social gathering, are you willing to be the one who expresses concern over attempted humor at others' expense?

Jeremiah spent years holding the line and remaining obedient to God while five kings of Judah rose and fell in Jerusalem from about 640 to 586 B.C. He saw the foreign powers of Assyria, Egypt, and Babylon wage war against his nation. Talk about hardship. He witnessed drought, famine, and siege. He experienced physical attacks and even got thrown into a deep muddy well. However, he never failed to ask for direction and follow through with what God instructed him to do. Are you willing to soldier on that way too?

Jeremiah's life may make yours look easier. After eight or so years under Jehoiakim's evil rule, Judah's uneasy alliance with Egypt waned. Babylon's King Nebuchadnezzar marched to take over Jerusalem, and Jehoiakim became his vassal for three years (2 Kings 24:1). Jeremiah and the others must have been reeling with the changes. What could they count on with enemies on all sides? When your government fails and invaders rotate like a revolving door, all semblance of normalcy vanishes.

Nebuchadnezzar made short work of Jehoiakim and another prince, both of whom rebelled, then he established Josiah's third son as his vassal. This Zedekiah played along for a while, but in his ninth year of rule, he bucked against Babylon. For the next year, around 584 B.C., Nebuchadnezzar encamped outside the walls and built siege works (2 Kings 25:1-2). He fully intended to punish the upstarts and dominate without mercy.

Can you relate to international events impacting your livelihood and lifestyle? Jeremiah had to be concerned how an invasion would affect his family and friends. Would anyone survive? Yet Jeremiah trusted God to work good for his loved ones.

While the Babylonians constructed scaffolding to scale the walls and battering rams to bash the gates, cheeky false prophets inside the city proclaimed, "You will not see the sword or suffer famine" (Jeremiah 14:13). These self-centered people found it inconceivable the majestic temple Solomon built to commemorate the golden era of their empire would ever fall.

This monument had stood for more than 350 years. The people of Judah prided themselves on the temple's sturdy cedar paneling carved with flowers (1 Kings 6:18). Gold adorned the altar and cherubim carvings decorated walls. The Jews fully expected God to pull another miracle and save them and their sacred building.

But God focused on their inner being. Previous success is no guarantee of future viability if people become arrogant. God does not reward disobedience. He wants believers who follow his commands rather than preen about his blessings.

Only Jeremiah warned that God's judgment was coming and defeat was imminent because the Israelites had forsaken their Lord. God would not allow the corruption of a symbolic monument to replace the temple of his peoples' hearts.

Are you clinging to anything other than God during your trial? If so, don't be surprised if he pries your fingers away from false supports. A job title, marital status, or bank account balance won't equal security without God as your Lord.

Jeremiah's candor didn't earn him popularity, and your truth-telling might be costly too. Temple leaders who resented Jeremiah's blunt prophecies of pending disaster beat him and put him in the stocks for public humiliation (Jeremiah 20:1-2). Sometimes, you have to stand for God, even if it hurts.

King Zedekiah started getting nervous as months dragged by and supplies dwindled. He sent messengers demanding Jeremiah inquire of the Lord. You wonder how far away Zedekiah had run because he depended on others to hear God for him. Though Jeremiah endured hardship, his reputation for integrity remained intact.

The Lord's response through Jeremiah wasn't encouraging. "Whoever stays in this city will die by the sword, famine or plague. But whoever goes out and surrenders to the Babylonians who are besieging you will live; they will escape with their lives" (Jeremiah 21:9).

God might shock you with his orders. He may direct a new course of action, which you resist as uncomfortable and downright unpleasant. Upheaval isn't fun, but there may be a deeper purpose.

Imagine being told to give up and go willingly to your enemy. That seems to contradict everything a brave people would do. However, God's disgust over Judah's willfulness mandated a fall. God had tried warnings, but he would take stronger measures to turn the people from their wickedness.

Jeremiah was caught in the middle. Again and again, he told his people to stop evil practices—such as burning children in sacrificial fires to idols—but the Israelites didn't pay attention (Jeremiah 32:35). For two years the Babylonian warriors cut off all food, and those trapped in Jerusalem slowly starved.

God dispatched Jeremiah to the front line. With loving devotion, Jeremiah accepted arduous duty. He reminded King Zedekiah the city would fall. Enraged by the continued doomsday forecast, Zedekiah imprisoned Jeremiah for discouraging the people (Jeremiah 32:1-5).

Hostile guards locked Jeremiah in the palace courtyard and labeled him a traitor. As they glared at him, he may have feared for his life from his own people. But he recalled God promised to make him a fortress to rise above the fray.

Perhaps you feel surrounded by issues. Adversaries in the workplace and negativity at home have walled you off from any reprieve. Allowing time for things to straighten out is exactly what you *don't* have. Take heart, though, because God's scheduling is sure. He may deny what you want for a time for a greater good. Listen carefully for him to explain how events will unfold and how you are to respond. Stay in prayer to hear his counsel. Like Jeremiah, God stays close to the faithful. He will deliver.

During a food shortage, death threats, certain defeat from invaders, and Zedekiah's royal displeasure, Jeremiah hears a surprising message from God. Jeremiah understands a cousin will arrive soon to ask Jeremiah to purchase family land in the territory of Benjamin (Jeremiah 32:6-7). Jeremiah must have scratched his head and wondered if he heard right. Why in the world would he buy land in an area the enemy controlled? What a crazy time to make an investment.

Would you provide capital for the title or pass on a seemingly shaky deal? In times where the economy resembles a bucking bronco at the rodeo, what do you do?

As a testimony to his faith, Jeremiah secured the deed with cash as soon as the cousin arrived. He asked others in the courtyard to witness the transaction and instructed them to preserve the sales documents in a clay jar. Jeremiah declared: "This is what the Lord Almighty, the God of Israel, says: Houses, fields and vineyards will again be bought in this land" (Jeremiah 32:15).

Jeremiah realized what the cousin didn't—God had set a time for correction, but he also scheduled redemption. The losses were temporary. Though God would allow the Babylonians to have victory to punish the Israelites' idolatry, after a 70-year period of discipline, God would gather his people from the foreign lands where they would be taken and bring them back to Jerusalem (Jeremiah 32:37-38).

A happy ending is what you want, but are you prepared to wait patiently—even decades—as God orchestrates events? Consider how he is crafting a legacy beyond your generation to include the well-being of future ones. God promised: "I will give them singleness of heart and action, so that they will always fear me and that all will then go well for them and for their children after them" (Jeremiah 32:39).

He wants followers to understand the severity of consequences for breaking the covenant. His people need to know he will not bless oppression of the poor nor shedding of innocent blood. God expects communities to be places of justice and compassion.

While you desire peace and prosperity, be alert to how God uses hardship to teach the right way to live. Though you may have done no wrong yourself, you might be caught up in circumstances like Jeremiah where more is at stake. God will not ignore a violation of his commands. People must realize their stubbornness requires him as a loving parent to step in and check wanton behavior.

Headstrong Zedekiah ignored years of warnings, and Nebuchadnezzar not only took him prisoner, but slaughtered Zedekiah's sons right in front of him (Jeremiah 39:6). Zedekiah's disobedience cost him the kingdom, as well as his family. Nebuchadnezzar also blinded Zedekiah, shackled him in bronze, and took him as a prize of war to Babylon (Jeremiah 39:7).

Unlike Zedekiah, trustworthy Jeremiah emerged from the ordeal with new opportunities. Nebuchadnezzar ordered his imperial guard to look after Jeremiah. "Don't harm him but do for him whatever he asks" (Jeremiah 39:12).

Do you wonder if spies repeated to Nebuchadnezzar during the months of siege one man alone inside the walls predicted Babylonian victory? Though Israelites shunned Jeremiah, God bestowed favor on him through foreign attackers. That's an unexpected irony for speaking the truth and following God's orders.

After Babylonian soldiers stormed the city, Nebuchadnezzar's commander of the Imperial Guard found Jeremiah chained among captives bound for exile to Babylon. The commander freed Jeremiah and gave him provisions (Jeremiah 40:1-5). The commander allowed Jeremiah to choose where he wanted to live.

Even if God takes you to a place of discomfort where the future is hard to see, he will protect you. You may not know when the trial will end, but you can be sure his ultimate goal for you is good. God said, "I will rejoice in doing them good and will assuredly plant them in this land with all my heart and soul" (Jeremiah 32:41).

Be like Jeremiah and invest in the future God lays out. God promises, "I will restore their fortunes" (Jeremiah 32:44). The wealth may not be material so much as the abundant peace of mind knowing you are living in a way that honors God. He will put a bronze wall around you. Confidence will secure you through many skirmishes.

God promises he will deliver you for a good purpose and make your enemies plead with you in times of disaster and distress (Jeremiah 15:11).

FOR REFLECTION

"I have made you a fortified city, an iron pillar and a bronze wall to stand against the whole land… They will fight against you but will not overcome you, for I am with you and will rescue you"
(Jeremiah 1:18-19).

Few U.S. citizens can relate to the experience of starvation due to siege or foreign invasion. These are calamities Jeremiah endured with the Israelites. Jeremiah's task was to call his people back to obedience to God and to encourage them to remain faithful.

In crisis, can people count on you to be strong and truthful? Consider listing effective leadership strategies you have seen to guide a nation or company during emergencies. How can these transfer to your family when experiencing a predicament? Like Jeremiah, hold fast to God and don't be afraid to speak what he tells you.

A PRAYER FOR TODAY

Dear Lord, Please train me to reflect before I speak. Please have your Holy Spirit teach me truth so the words out of my mouth build your kingdom with love and respect. Instruct me when to remain silent in prayer and when to speak up boldly for what is right. Please make me a fortified city that doesn't bow to deceptive pressures. Amen

Chapter Four

BANQUETING ON DELICIOUS CRUMBS

$\mathcal{E}$ver been to an all-you-can-eat buffet piled high with tempting dishes? Roast beef awaits you under a toasty warming light, while nearby sushi rolls distract you with tiny slivers of celery wrapped with pink salmon. Potato salad with pickles and Waldorf with crunchy, crisp green apples beckon across the aisle. You inspect another diner's loaded tray and wonder where to find the fat yeast rolls with butter dripping down the sides. (Bet you're hungry now, even if you weren't before.) And that's not even gliding past the dessert display with powder-sugared chocolate chip brownies, red cherry tarts, and a soft-serve vanilla ice cream machine.

Unfortunately, you don't get to eat any of the delicious entrees or sides. You aren't even invited to the feast. In a tight back corner, you watch restaurant staff bustle by as seated people tuck napkins in their collars and smack their lips in anticipation of the fabulous food. Your stomach growls and you fidget. Invisible to all, you hope someone might notice and wave you over to a place beside him.

That sense of emptiness amid plenty might be how a woman in Jesus' time felt. Her story is described in only a few verses by both Matthew and Mark, yet her encounter with Jesus reveals powerful insights about what he will do for us if we pursue him. Our mystery lady never is named. The only way she is identified is by the regions where she grew up and lived. Matthew calls her a Canaanite, while Mark says Syrophoenician. Either way, the lady didn't come from the best part of Jerusalem. She didn't have the stamp of approval as a certified Jew. The Bible doesn't say how she got to Tyre, nor why she traveled without a husband in a world dominated by males. But what the scriptures make clear is she had a huge hunger for Jesus' help.

To backtrack a bit, after Jesus fed the 5,000 and walked on the Sea of Galilee, word spread quickly when he arrived in Gennesaret. "And when the men of that place recognized Jesus, they sent word to all the surrounding country" (Matthew 14:35). News traveled fast. The miracle worker was nearby and loved ones could be healed. The lady mobilizes to find this one whom everyone says can do the impossible.

While common people flock to him to relieve their agony, the Pharisees from Jerusalem saunter out to quibble about how to wash hands. Jesus chides them that being unclean isn't about man-made rituals but about what's in a person's heart (Matthew 15:11). The disciples get nervous because Jesus is offending the elite teachers, and Jesus gets frustrated with the bunch for being dull. He leaves and go to an area near Tyre and Sidon (Matthew 15:21).

That's where he encounters the lady. No physical description of her is given, but her heart must have shone like a beacon. While the Pharisees approached him in arrogance, she cried out in need and fell at Jesus' feet. "Lord, Son of David, have mercy on me! My daughter is demon-possessed and suffering terribly" (Matthew 15:22).

Oddly enough, Jesus pretended he didn't hear her. The disciples, growing uncomfortable at the scene she was making, urged Jesus to send her away. Ever been at a low point yourself and the very people you thought would stand with you turn away in embarrassment? Has Jesus seemed distant and deaf to your pleas? His hearing is just fine, and he cares. He might just be testing *your* level of commitment. Do you truly believe he has the answer you seek? He doesn't enjoy religious debates, which skim the surface of propriety and never examine bedrock principles of God, such as compassion.

The woman wasn't afraid to shout and call attention to herself. She didn't seem to care what the crowd whispered about her. Her sole focus was on the person who could restore her darling to a healthy child who could run and play again. She envisioned her daughter back in glowing health with rosy cheeks, curls bouncing, and no more shuddering from the oppression of ruthless demons.

A Pharisee might argue demons only possess those who have sinned, but how many children toy with evil? Modern science would have you believe devilish creatures exist only in movies. Take heed because the Bible indicates otherwise. Just as the man born blind in John 9 would glorify Jesus' ability to restore sight, so perhaps this little girl's plight would teach others of his kindness and power. "This happened so that the works of God might be displayed" (John 9:3).

The determined momma stares at Jesus and waits. She will stay at his feet all day waiting for him to notice her. She will do anything for her baby.

Jesus' reply turns upside down everything we usually hear about him in Sunday School. He doesn't rush to her side and brush away her tears. Nor does he immediately reassure her. Jesus doesn't ask the child's name or age. "First let the children eat all they want, for it is not right to take the children's bread and toss it to the dogs" (Mark 7:27).

That statement sounded as if Jesus had lost sight of what was going on. He wouldn't speak disparagingly of a hurting soul, would he? Good grief. Why would he bring up dogs at all as though the woman were a cur unworthy of his attention? Matthew's version said Jesus answered, "I was sent only to the lost sheep of Israel" (Matthew 15:24). Did the woman's heart sink in defeat, realizing she wasn't part of the "in" group?

Maybe the Jews in the crowd lifted their chins in superiority and dusted off their robes from possible contamination by this uncouth Gentile. If only you could see the woman's face. Did she look away and make ready to depart?

Instead, she could have squared her shoulders as the burning flame of devotion ignited her bravery. She recalled leaving her daughter tossing with fever and whimpering on torn bedding. This mother hadn't come all the way to be told no, not when her child's life depended on a courageous stand. Possibly her mind's eye flashed back to home where her Canaan dog kept vigil.[1] The woman counted on it watching over the livestock and children. No yappy lap pup, this ancient breed patrolled the grounds and kept out predators.

On many mornings, the woman remembered seeing her daughter at the breakfast table "sneaking" snacks to the gentle guardian. Her daughter would giggle as the dog's muzzle tickled the palm of her hand. This lady's canine was no mangy mutt, and neither was she. Picture her throwing a thick mahogany braid over her shoulder and raising a heart-shaped chin. In a culture where women weren't encouraged to speak, she comes right back at Jesus with a challenge in a cool, calm voice.

"Lord, even the dogs under the table eat the children's crumbs," she replied (Mark 7:28). Can't you just hear the gasps of surprise from the men observing them? How dare a simple woman from impure lineage speak so forthrightly to Jesus?

Some might think she was speaking poorly of herself. However, if you've ever seen a beloved house pet wait patiently in the kitchen for the tasty tidbit sure to come, you understand the woman may have actually referenced the privileged position of a trusted companion. Back in the day, only the most cherished work animal would be allowed inside with family. The woman might have implied she too would abide quietly until the master shared freely what was on his table. She would relish what he offered and be grateful.

Would Jesus be offended at her persistence and brush her off? You wish the Bible described Jesus' expression. Maybe he had a twinkle in his eye and tried to stifle the grin tugging at the corner of his mouth.

---

1 American Kennel Club, "About the Canaan Dog," https://www.akc.org/dog-breeds/canaan-dog/.

Maybe he threw his head back and laughed outright in delight at her refreshing faith.

Her pluckiness demolished any need for theological debates. She knew God had more than enough food, and she knew he was good. She didn't get sidetracked in stereotypes or genealogy. Just as she advocated for her little girl, she knew her heavenly Father looked out for her. Even God's "crumbs" are so filling and rich no other banquet can compare.

Then Jesus told her, "For such a reply, you may go; the demon has left your daughter" (Mark 7:29). No sirens went off, nor did any fanfare follow the announcement. The Canaanite woman took Jesus at his word. Her smile of gratitude must have been a beautiful sight. The way she sprang up and had a skip in her step must have brought Jesus joy. While others nitpicked his teaching, this woman petitioned with her whole heart and mind. Her daughter was healed.

God also invites you to his banquet. He will demolish any labels or untrue messages of "not good enough." You are welcome at his table where abundance overflows. "Taste and see that the Lord is good; blessed is the one who takes refuge in him" (Psalm 34:8).

The heavily laden banquet table is set with a spotless white linen cloth and beeswax candles glow softly. Silver service flanks the best china plates. Jesus pulls out the chair for you as the guest of honor and invites you to sit beside him. Then he offers you the best of everything.

Please pass the golden macaroni and cheese … and the green beans with toasted almonds … and the prime rib au jus. Save space for the carrot cake frosted with fluffy cream cheese. And invite others you know to share in the feast. No reservations necessary.

God promises he will rain down bread from heaven for you. You are to go out each day and gather enough for that day (Exodus 16:4).

FOR REFLECTION

"Then Jesus said to his host, 'When you give a luncheon or dinner, do not invite your friends, your brothers or sisters, your relatives, or your rich neighbors; if you do, they may invite you back and so you will be repaid. But when you give a banquet, invite the poor, the crippled, the lame, the blind, and you will be blessed. Although they cannot repay you, you will be repaid at the resurrection of the righteous'" (Luke 14:12-13).

In Luke 14, a prominent Pharisee invited Jesus to eat at his house one Sabbath after Jesus had performed many miracles. Milling around, Jesus noticed guests vying for seats of honor. He explained how humility is an important trait, then advised his host to include people who needed his generosity, rather than those of equal social standing. This connects to where the Canaanite woman sought blessing, not because she "deserved" it, but because she trusted God's goodness. Recall times someone has included you in a gathering and made you feel welcome. Whom can you invite as a guest to show kindness?

A PRAYER FOR TODAY

Dear Lord, Thank you for the invitation to be with you. I am never alone. You invite me to a place of plenty where all my needs are met. I am grateful for your provisions. Please help me see others in need and be willing to share what I have freely. Amen

Chapter Five

EXPANSIVE ACCOUNTING

Cash flow might be as tight as swimming holes for tadpoles in Tucson's dry season. Rent's overdue, hospital bills climb, and the bank account balance is skinnier than a paperclip. You wonder how to keep up when the nest egg falls and shatters at the base of the money tree. These earthly concerns are legitimate and immediate, but there is a financier who audits and has everything under control.

Jesus gave Peter a lesson in bookkeeping while they were in Capernaum. Tax collectors pigeon-holed the disciple alone asking, "Doesn't your teacher pay the temple tax?" (Matthew 17:24). No one knows if these agents asked Jesus to pay up. Maybe they feared him. Maybe they suspected they had no way to pressure him. So they went after Peter instead. Peter probably gulped and straightened his tunic, stalling how to answer. He knew their band had limited resources and stayed on the move to minister to large crowds.

Peter may have craned his neck to scope out where Judas was to wave him over with the communal purse. The disciple might have turned out his pockets, empty except for lint, and grinned sheepishly. The follower knew laws in Exodus commanded all Jews to support the temple with annual taxes. He didn't know how—or when—Jesus would settle the obligation. With feeding thousands and healing hundreds, the guys had been a bit busy. But Peter understood the enforcers wouldn't forgive late payments.

He could have held up a hand with a wait-just-a-moment motion and backed away a bit. "Yes, he does," Peter answered (Matthew 17:25). Then he departed to let Jesus know they had a problem.

Do you go to Jesus for advice on how to handle money and invite him to sit at the desk with you to sort bills? He is happy to help calculate debts and align income. His awareness isn't so caught up in the heavenlies he does not know about earthly obligations.

Jesus wasn't at all surprised to see Peter return home with his thick brows furrowed and his complexion pale. Jesus asked Peter right away, "From whom do the kings of the earth collect duty and taxes—from their own children or from others?" (Matthew 17:25).

Peter probably groaned inwardly, thinking to himself, *Here he goes again with another one of those darned parables. We need to figure out how to get money fast, or we're going to debtor's prison for tax evasion. I don't have time for these puzzles from my master. The temple police could come knocking any moment.*

Taking a deep breath, Peter considered Jesus' question. Kings certainly didn't tax their own kids. Royal family members lived in luxury and had every advantage. Of course, lowly subjects were the ones to pay tribute and support royalty. Peter answered, "From others" (Matthew 17:26).

Unruffled, Jesus drove home his logic. "Then the children are exempt" (Matthew 17:26).

In healthy families, members look after each other. Parents support young children, and later, grown-up offspring look after elderly adults. The idea taxes are required to ensure needs are met is nonsensical in a loving environment. How silly to expect a father would collect taxes from his beloved children. God's largesse has no limit. All he asks is for his children to be wise stewards of the gifts he entrusts to their care. He doesn't supply wanton desires, but delights in sharing good gifts for stability.

In recognition of these presents, God had directed Moses more than a thousand years prior that his people would commit money toward helping others. From the poverty of slavery in Egypt, God wanted them to remember regularly everything came from him, including their lives. "The Lord said to Moses, 'When you take a census of the Israelites to count them, each one must pay the Lord a ransom for his life" (Exodus 30:11-12).

This payment tradition established them as God's people. Not only did their financial well-being depend on him, but so did their bodies for every breath. God continued his guidance of Moses saying, "Receive the atonement money from the Israelites and use it for the service of the tent of meeting. It will be a memorial for the Israelites before the Lord, making atonement for your lives" (Exodus 30:16).

Atonement isn't a word you hear much today, but one explanation of it from ancient Hebrew is the idea of covering errors, according to Jeff A. Benner.[2] Jesus is your guarantor. He will satisfy any outstanding charges of sin you cannot pay. He buffers you from debt collectors, particularly regarding mistakes you've made that must be reconciled. While Peter grappled with the literal level he needed quick cash to pay the bill, Jesus hinted at a deeper spiritual realm. Jesus would sacrifice himself to ensure everyone else in the family owed nothing. His inheritance would transfer without encumbrances, or burdens, because Jesus prepaid anything owed with his life by choosing to die on the cross.

Jesus' estate planning is so thorough. He makes arrangements not only for the future but also for what's needed right now. He said to Peter, "But so that we may not cause offense, go to the lake and throw out your line" (Matthew 17:27).

As a former fisherman, Peter knew money could be earned. Though he might have doubted he could catch enough on one line

---

2 Jeff A. Benner, "Atonement," Ancient Hebrew Research Center, https://www.ancient-hebrew. org/definition/atonement.htm#:~:text=The%20Hebrew%20word%20kaphar%20means,is%20 often%20translated%20as%20atonement.&text=We%20express%20this%20idea%20 through,that%20covers%20over%20the%20error.

for the temple tax, he was game to try because he'd seen Jesus do many amazing things already. Besides, going fishing might not be such a bad idea to get away for a little while.

Peter grabbed his equipment and started toward the door when Jesus added, "Take the first fish you catch; open its mouth and you will find a four-drachma coin. Take it and give it to them for my tax and yours" (Matthew 17:27).

Alrighty, Peter probably thought as he strode toward the nearby Sea of Galilee, also known as Lake Tiberias and Israel's largest freshwater lake.[3] *If the boss says there'll be a fish, then there will be. Who am I to question the one who walks on water and talks with Elijah on the mountain?*

With each encounter with God, you develop more faith and trust. Each time you step out and expect him to work miracles—however he deems appropriate—you see him move in surprising ways. Maybe Peter whistled as he settled the fishing equipment up on his shoulder and pondered what Jesus would do this time.

Do you also anticipate deliverance? Do you recall the many ways rescue already has occurred? An unexpected check arrives in the nick of time. A bill is cancelled. A friend loans you an item needed so you don't have to buy it. Jesus doesn't disappoint.

Keep your eyes open to possibilities. Peter had to wonder how one fish would show up on his line with a silver coin inside its mouth. How unlikely. Yet Peter had seen too much to ignore the opportunity. Speculation is intriguing.

One modern traveler to Israel researched the possibility of such an occurrence as Jesus foretold. David Q. Hall writes that local fishermen around Lake Tiberias say there is a type of fish resembling tilapia in the region. This species is known "to carry its small young in its

---

3 NASA Earth Observatory, "Lake Tiberias (Sea of Galilee), Northern Israel," https://earthobservatory.nasa.gov/images/40147/lake-tiberias-sea-of-galilee-northern-israel#:~:text=Israel's%20largest%20freshwater%20lake%2C%20Lake,meters%20(141%20feet)%20deep.

Chapter Six

SHAME SHIELDED BY GRACE

*P*sssst. Look down. The zipper is open on your trousers. (Hate to tell you, but figure you'd rather know than be embarrassed.)

And ma'am, that missing button on your blouse has left a gaping hole, just where you don't want it.

Sliding lingerie, trailing toilet paper under heels, and vanishing swimsuits make for clothing nightmares. Being exposed isn't fun. Two stories in the Bible's first book reveal how to handle such fashion mishaps with grace.

Early in Genesis, Adam and Eve are blithe streakers. They haven't a care in the world. Until they are disobedient and do what God asked them not to—chow on the forbidden fruit. "Then the eyes of both of them were opened, and they realized they were naked; so they sewed fig leaves together and made coverings for themselves" (Genesis 3:7).

You may have been tempted too. You sample a cigarette and start an addiction. Maybe pornography starts with one picture burned on your memory. But the media hype about hidden "pleasures" tastes as foul as buzzard bile. The reality of being deceived deflates you, and you simmer in regret. Full of shame, you think you can hide the misstep from God and come up with a genius plan for a cover up. Like you can do that with God. Duh.

Adam and Eve grabbed leaves and scrambled to make coverings for themselves. Just then, they heard God walking in the cool of the day toward them. "Quick. Hide in here," Eve may have hissed to Adam, pulling him toward a tree.

"Where are you?" the Lord called to the man (Genesis 3:9).

Adam leaned his torso from around the trunk and answered, "I heard you in the garden, and I was afraid because I was naked; so I hid" (Genesis 3:10).

You can imagine God shaking his head with disappointment. He knew they had broken the rules, but he gave them an opportunity to come clean with him. "Who told you that you were naked? Have you eaten from the tree that I commanded you not to eat from?" (Genesis 3:11).

Instead of shouldering responsibility and admitting the error, Adam blamed Eve. She pointed to the serpent coiled with its tongue flickering in a suppressed evil laugh. God's plan for a peaceful existence for all in a beautiful garden crashes with selfish desires.

God deals out discipline for all three: the snake forever more will be lowly and crawl on its belly. Eve will have pain in childbearing and be ruled over by her husband. Adam will be sentenced to painful toil on a cursed land (Genesis 3:14-19). Once the punishments are meted out, you would think God would walk away and withdraw his presence. But he doesn't.

He cares for them by clothing them and covering their shame. "The Lord God made garments of skin for Adam and his wife and clothed them" (Genesis 3:21). You can infer innocent animals died to resolve Adam and Eve's sin. A sacrifice had to be made to atone for their willful choices. A leopard lies motionless while God traces his fingers over the sleek pelt. Then God sighs and fashions the lifeless soft fur into a tunic. Wonder if tears rolled down God's cheeks as he made such an alteration in the paradise he'd envisioned.

Have you seen others harmed by someone else's blatant disregard for rules? Whole communities crash when even one person slides into sin and undermines trust.

God holds rule-breakers accountable with consequences, and he will expect a reckoning. However, he won't abandon you nor shame you about poor decisions. "A broken and contrite heart, O God, you will not despise" (Psalm 51:17). He will quietly meet your need and help you move forward to a new level of responsibility.

Just as God covers shame with his loving grace, so you may need to deal with the sins of others. An example of this is found with Noah in Genesis. Though a righteous and blameless man (Genesis 6:9), Noah got himself in a pickle after the ark landed. He got drunk. And not just a bit tipsy. "When he drank some of its wine (the new land's grapes), he became drunk and lay uncovered inside his tent" (Genesis 9:21).

Maybe he tried to escape the nightmarish memories of people crying out to him from the flood waters. Perhaps he couldn't shake the sorrow of seeing the whole world devastated. He could have underestimated the wine's effect, but the result was him buck naked and not in his right mind.

His youngest son, Ham, barreled in the tent and saw his dad in this compromised state. Instead of being discrete and taking care of his dad, he went outside and told his two brothers. They, however, acted in discretion. "But Shem and Japheth took a garment and laid it across their shoulders; then they walked in backward and covered their father's nakedness" (Genesis 9:23).

Is there someone you have observed in a delicate position? If so, what did you do? Hopefully, you covered their regret and shame with kindness and sensitivity. You protected their vulnerability until they were strong enough to remedy the situation themselves. Like Shem and Japheth, your face "turned the other way so that they would not see their father naked" (Genesis 9:23).

Disrespecting others' weakness will cause alienation. "When Noah awoke from his wine and found out what his youngest son had done to him, he said, 'Cursed be Canaan.'" (Genesis 9:25). That rift divided the family for centuries.

How long do you think your unkindness may affect others? Not being able to overcome a debilitating mistake can affect generations. How blessed are those who extend grace quietly and shore up others who have fallen.

Though you don't want to ignore problems, you also don't want an attitude of judgment and superiority to push away someone who needs help. Let God hold them accountable in his time and his way. Meanwhile, avert your eyes from their shame and offer a blanket of loving support to cover them until they can stand upright again. "My brothers and sisters, if one of you should wander from the truth and someone should bring that person back, remember this: Whoever turns a sinner from the error of their way will save them from death and cover a multitude of sins" (James 5:19-20).

You can't know the pain someone is under. Be willing to help shoulder their burden. Remember how Jesus covered all shame when he sacrificed himself. God sees the purity of Jesus when we turn our lives and mistakes over to his son for redemption.

God promises he will walk with you and be your God and that you will be his (Leviticus 26:12).

FOR REFLECTION

"Guard my life and rescue me; do not let me be put to shame, for I take refuge in you. May integrity and uprightness protect me, because my hope, Lord, is in you." (Psalm 25:20-21)

Think of an embarrassing moment you've had where someone recognized your discomfort and covered for you. How does the grace of God overlook your indiscretions to give you a chance to regroup? Does your critical eye on others need to be softened with the same compassion you've received?

A PRAYER FOR TODAY

Dear Lord, I am ashamed of many things. Though I try to block memories of where I've fallen short, I realize you know. There are no secrets between us. Thank you for the spotless covering Jesus provided through his sacrifice to blot out my sins. I am sorry for my willfulness. Please help me develop your eyes of compassion when I view others. I want to be a vessel of kindness rather than condemnation because you've forgiven me. Amen

Chapter Seven

STUBBORN MINING

*Y*ou. Don't. Care. Period. Gave up on all sentimental silliness a while back. Caring is too costly. Though you know the Bible teaches forgiveness and forgetting the past, you are wounded in deep places. Rather than trust again and make yourself vulnerable, you have developed a force field of protection that would rival the TV. Captain Kirk's star ship *USS Enterprise* under attack from Klingons.

Hurtling through the atmosphere, you ignore what could be because you are too busy counting all the never-did-happens or shouldn't-have-happeneds. Feeling like jettisoned space junk, you flee failed relationships. A friend disappears. A marriage unravels or a child takes off or a date ghosts away. You isolate and give up, but in doing so, part of you dies. The flight pattern leaves you adrift in a starless black void.

It's chilly in this self-imposed exile, and there's freezer burn on your heart. Not that you want to be a loner, but you don't know how to reconnect safely. However, you aren't in this journey alone. God observes your restless wandering and desires to restore you to fellowship. "I will give them an undivided heart and put a new spirit in them," God promised the Israelites who had drifted far away from him (Ezekiel 11:19). He will do the same for you. If there is loss, he redeems. In disappointment, he sows hope. For loneliness, he establishes friendships.

"I will remove from them their heart of stone and give them a heart of flesh" (Ezekiel 11:19). Rock works well in some situations, like felling giants, but not so much for personal connections. Encasing feelings under rigid control prevents intimacy. Though opening up to others is desirable, when you have layers of pain to work through, trust doesn't come easily.

Just as the earth forms layers of valuable materials hidden below the surface, so can you mine experiences to extract useful insights. Dressed granite in the building world is "considered a prestigious material used to influence others because of its elegance, durability and quality."[7] The same can be true for you, if you learn to move past aches and unrealistic expectations. This requires concerted effort and focus.

According to Geology Science, "Granite crystallizes from silica-rich magmas that are miles deep in Earth's crust."[8] Over time with heat and pressure, minerals "cook" into strong substances studded with quartz and feldspar. Light and dark shades give the natural stone its attractive appearance, as can life experiences make a person more appealing to others. Few can relate to perfection, but most can connect with a person who has made mistakes and been able to regroup with wisdom and acceptance.

The choice of what you do with the raw material is up to you. Some might construct a towering tombstone and memorialize a screwup, thereby overshadowing any future. Others may choose to lay a solid flooring with great endurance no matter how much traffic. Another builder may use granite to decorate a kitchen counter because it is durable and heat resistant and will be the site of many fulfilling meals. How do you want to utilize your life experiences? Are you going to continue hiding hurts in a simmering subterranean vein, or do you want to quarry lessons learned and move forward?

Some of the most delightful people in the world are the ones who have been molded by hardship and still see the sparkle in life.

---

7 *Geology Science, "Granite," 2021, https://geologyscience.com/rocks/granite/* .
8 Ibid.

They usher in laughter at just the right moment and hold your hand when no words will do. They don't chatter during your suffering but stand stalwartly beside you in a comforting presence. These wondrous encouragers show you can refuse to let circumstances crush you. They reveal how to find joy and form your own unique pattern with all the colorful variations of life's happenstances.

These special mentors are the ones who meet you with a giggle about a faux pas instead of a gasp. They chuckle at your consternation and gently guide you to see what appeared a tragedy is no big deal. Affirmers see you as you are and don't constrict you into a tiny mold that doesn't fit. These supporters hold you accountable, but also are the first to rush to your defense.

Fellowship is where long-term strength can be found. "Give, and it will be given to you. A good measure, pressed down, shaken together and running over, will be poured into your lap. For with the measure you use, it will be measured to you" (Luke 6:38). Shared experiences enrich both parties when God is at the center. Try meeting for a walk around the lake. Invite someone to chat over coffee. Build a relationship in baby steps. One time, you may reach out to someone who needs a friend. Next time, someone may return the favor.

Sometimes to have a friend, you have to be one first. God may lead you to unlikely connections. Acts 9 recounts the story of the dangerous Saul hunting down Jesus converts, only to be blinded on the way to Damascus. Saul's attacks were arrested with a divine encounter. For three days, Saul hunkered down in despair, not knowing what to do or where to turn. But when Saul prayed, God mobilized Ananias in a vision. Understandably, Ananias felt reluctant to pay a call to a formidable adversary.

"I have heard many reports about this man and all the harm he has done to your holy people in Jerusalem," Ananias said to God. "And he has come here with authority from the chief priests to arrest all who call on your name" (Acts 9:13-14). Ananias knew this call would be no picnic. He feared for his life.

Fun social outings are easy. Go fishing and trade the biggest catch stories. Or go clothes shopping and admire new fashions. But meet a scary guy who has traumatized and imprisoned many? No way. That couldn't be friendship. Or could it? God has funny ideas how he wants his people to look after each other. He sees below the surface and wants us to do the same.

God didn't tolerate Ananias' waffling. "Go. This man is my chosen instrument to proclaim my name to the Gentiles and their kings and to the people of Israel. I will show him how much he must suffer for my name" (Acts 9:15-16).

Maybe Ananias grumbled and shuffled off. Maybe he saluted and made a crisp turnabout. Either way, he went directly to Straight Street and found Saul. Ananias placed his hands on Saul. "Brother Saul, the Lord—Jesus, who appeared to you on the road as you were coming here—has sent me so that you may see again and be filled with the Holy Spirit" (Acts 9:17).

In times of pain when you falter, who has come alongside to support you? When hard times knocked you down, who lifted you? Ananias teaches friendship starts with obedience to God to love others. In one season, a person may have more to give than another. God arranges opportunities for friendships, but you must choose to cultivate them. Who could you call to drive you home from the emergency room at midnight? The bigger question is are you willing to be that person for someone else?

Imagine the joy in Saul's eyes when the scales fell off and the first face he saw was Ananias'. What gratitude and peace must have filled that moment after days of dark despair. Saul's change of heart must have been glorious. He saw God's deliverance and had his own faith bolstered by being part of a miracle. Within a few days, Saul astonished listeners as he convincingly preached in the synagogue Jesus was the Son of God. Friendship has the power to affect many lives. Taking a first step requires trusting God to lead you to the right people at the right time.

The net kingdom result of these alliances goes far beyond the immediate fellowship to impact whole communities. Another story about friendship in Acts 9 shares how a disciple named Tabitha always did good and helped the poor. Like Ananias, she took initiative to connect with people. In her town of Joppa, she didn't wait for someone to reach out to her. She lived life to the fullest and expressed her kindness in deeds for many.

When a sudden illness took her life, her friends washed and placed her body in an upper room. However, her friends weren't willing to let her go. These disciples dispatched two men to find Peter and urge him to help. Traveling nearby, Peter responded to their pleas and veered off to see what was going on. In the room where Tabitha's body lay, widows stood crying and displaying the clothing Tabitha had made for them while she was alive.

This was the era before ready-made outfits and online ordering. Widows, often left with little financial support, depended on the charity of others to be well dressed. Imagine Peter's eyes scanning the crowd of teary-eyed women as they clutched colorful dresses with tiny hand stitches. Tabitha's hours of loving tailoring showed.

Maybe to give himself peace to think, Peter shooed them all out of the room. He got down on his knees and prayed. Note again the power of prayer when God is invited into the equation. Peter turned toward her body saying, "Tabitha, get up" (Acts 9:40).

She opened her eyes and sat up. Maybe she patted her hair into place and smoothed her robes. "Where is everyone?" she might have asked. "I must have dozed off."

Shouts of joy and rounds of hugs must have ushered in Tabitha's reunion with her friends. God rewarded their faith and restored her to them. Their love wasn't the selfish type of control, but shared uplifting where they helped each other grow stronger.

He will guide you to those whom you can fortify on their journey. Our Lord also will dispatch others to bring you back to wholeness when you feel weary or stumped. God ordains a unity bringing him glory and draws others into his caring family. Like Ananias, take a holy detour to make a new acquaintance. No telling how God will bless the interaction.

God promises he will give you an undivided heart, remove the heart of stone, and give you a heart of flesh to care and be obedient (Ezekiel 11:19).

FOR REFLECTION

"A friend loves at all times, and a brother is born for a time of adversity" (Proverbs 17:17).

Being a friend in a delightful season is easy, but you identify friends when they stand with you, even when you have nothing to give.

Who has been the "Ananias" in your life? Consider how that person looked beyond your shortcomings to see what you could become. What characteristics do you look for in a friend? How many of these do you exhibit for others? Think about who God may send you to. Do you have a story to tell about an "unlikely" contact who blessed you mightily? Consider what happened along the way to solidify the partnership.

A PRAYER FOR TODAY

Dear Lord, It boggles my mind you would call me friend. I appreciate the way we can talk together any time, any place. I pray you would give me courage like Ananias and Peter to do uncomfortable things to support others facing hardship. Please help my faith grow, so I can encourage others in their faith walk. Amen

Chapter Eight

HE LOVES YOU STILL

*Y*ou feel ugly when you look in the mirror. Dark circles underscore deadpan eyes and the only remnant of a smile are frown lines. You blink and hope when you open your eyes again the sad image will transform. Not so much. Superimposed images from glossy magazines of handsome men and gorgeous women mock your average face. You run a hand through limp hair and sigh. Who would ever want someone like you?

God does because He is head-over-heels about you, just as you are. The heavenly Father will scale the highest snow-topped mountain and dive into the coldest indigo ocean to find you and bring you to him in a huge bear hug. He won't let go, no matter how much you wriggle or try to scoot away because you feel unworthy of his affection. In your heart, you might think, *If God only knew what I'd done, he'd never take me back home with him.*

News flash: God already knows your history. He's seen every shameful act and heard every lie. He's not naïve. He still wants you. His desire hasn't cooled nor has his devotion waned.

You don't have to make yourself presentable before he will notice you. In fact, he desires you even in your most unattractive moments. His affection for you isn't conditional. Let a woman with a tainted reputation tell you how God redeemed her.

৩ ৩ ৩ ৩ ৩

My name is Gomer. Some say my name means "complete" in Hebrew.[9] I would agree—as in complete idiot. I wanted to be beautiful and spent lots of time styling my long, ebony hair and choosing sexy outfits. I had guys watching every sway of my hips and loved the attention. Their whistles and catcalls were music to my ears and made my pouty ruby red lips smirk. The only problem was my desire for center stage didn't stop there. Tottering around on high heels tripped me up in more ways than one.

Maybe the wine went to my head one night. Maybe I just let down my guard too much, but in the morning, I woke up next to a guy whose name I couldn't remember. His bad breath almost knocked me out, and his leer made me feel filthy. How could I have fallen so far? I edged to the far side of the bed and looked for my clothes. Daylight flooded the apartment with every sordid detail of discarded apparel littering the worn carpet. I sat up, smelling the odor of unwashed bodies and clutched the wrinkled sheet to my bosom.

My head hammered with pain, and my mouth felt full of cotton balls. I slid my feet to the floor and noticed my French manicured toenails didn't look so sexy. I wondered how quickly I could get dressed. No way to go home without the entire neighborhood seeing me leave. Surely I couldn't stay where I was, with the neanderthal burping and scratching his hairy torso. All I wanted to do was get out of there as fast as possible. Unfortunately, a quick escape wasn't to be.

"Where do you think you're going?" the guy sneered. "I shelled out a lot of dough last night buying you those fruity cocktails. I want my money's worth." His calloused hand yanked me backward, and I was too weak to stop him. The evening's Prince Charming turned into a monster.

Later, when he went to work, I made it home. Only there was no warm reception. I don't blame my parents. The fault was mine. They had been up all night frantic with worry. The kitchen looked like a

---

9 Mike Campbell, "Behind the Name," https://www.behindthename.com/name/gomer.

disaster zone with half-full coffee cups and dark spills dribbled on the usually pristine counter. My folks called neighbors and friends to search for me. Every hour of their vigil fueled terror, which turned into anger when I sauntered home all disheveled and barefoot. The telltale sparkly dress shoe with the broken heel in my hand and the smeared mascara told them all they cared to know.

Though relieved I was alive, their disapproval hurt worse than anything. I had ignored their wise counsel, and now there was a penalty to pay. "How could you do this to us?" my mom yelled. My friends hung their heads and wouldn't meet my gaze. They didn't want to have anything to do with me either. I had gone too far. Disgraced, I ran into my bedroom and slammed the door. Then I packed a few things and snuck outside so I wouldn't have to see any more disappointed looks. I went back to the guy because there was nowhere else to go.

Shame haunted me because vanity caused my downfall. Well, I was dirty now and nothing could make me clean. Not the long, hot shower. Not the fresh outfit. Not even the perfume could cover the stench of my self-loathing. Accepting I was no longer worthy of anything good, I settled for a life of dark nights and blacker dawns. That was what I deserved.

Things got worse. The guy I was with got more abusive. Trapped, I didn't know what to do. Then in a moment of absolute despair, I prayed God would deliver me. A few days went by and I thought, *Great. Not even God can stand me.* Then a strange thing happened. As I walked down the sidewalk, a nice-looking man in a suit smiled and said a shy "hello." For the next few weeks, we kept running into each other. After a month, he invited me to sit with him on the park bench. That's where he proposed. Can you believe it?

Wanting to come clean, I told him my sad story. He said he already knew, and God had told him to take care of me. I wasn't sure if the gentleman was the nutcase or if I was, but I wouldn't let the opportunity slip away. We got married and things were good. I mean, really good. He gave me a nice home and brought daisies for me to arrange. I felt secure and loved. He gave me white gold earrings and bracelets with diamonds and took me out to a dinner date at least once a week. Our love seemed solid.

Fast forward four years and three children arrived. We had a son, then a daughter, then another son. My husband seemed distracted by his career. I got lost in all the mommying. My husband offered to babysit when he got home from work so I could go to the gym for some *me* time a few nights a week. I met a hunk with a suave smile who said sweet things to tickle my ego. This new acquaintance also wore a wedding ring. I thought our banter was harmless.

After a couple months, my gym buddy and I got kale-spinach smoothies at the place next to the gym. One thing led to another. You would think I had learned my lesson about lust, but I gave into temptation again and cheated. This broke all the promises I'd made to my husband and myself. Infidelity hurt my spouse and harmed my children.

What kind of an awful person was I? I ran away from home and hid in a cheap hotel, all the while berating myself for being foolish. I couldn't go back to my husband. I'd already done too much damage.

Imagine my shock when I heard a loud knock. I looked through the scratched peephole to see my husband standing outside with a bunch of red roses. I opened the door. His shaven jaw was firm and his eyes were clear. "Gomer, I love you. There is nothing you can do to change that. I want you to come home."

I gulped and couldn't believe he still wanted me after the horrible things I'd done.

He added, "The kids and I miss you. The house feels empty without you."

I wanted to shout and wrap my arms around his neck, but all I could mumble was, "You don't have to do this. I let you down and I'm so sorry."

He said, "When I made a covenant with you, that is forever. You've hurt me terribly, and I don't know how we will work through everything, but I am willing to try if you are." He stepped forward, set the flowers on the table, and enfolded me in the gentlest hug. As my tears soaked his shirt, he held on and stroked my hair.

When I finally got myself together, I looked up and whispered, "You love me that much?"

He let go and backed up a bit. Then he looked me right in the eye. "Never doubt how much I love you." He reached for my hand. Then he helped gather my few belongings and carried them to the car. "We've got a lot of healing ahead of us, but you are my beloved. Nothing will ever change that."

I sought a counselor for help to deal with my issues, and we saw a couples' therapist. I had an appointment with our family doctor to be tested for sexually-transmitted diseases and waited anxiously for results. The next months were full of soul-searching and rebuilding. But with God's help, we found a way to reignite our flame and restore trust. With time, we also rediscovered a tender physical intimacy.

A year later, we had a ceremony to renew our vows. Our minister led us to recite Hosea 2:19-20:

> *I will betroth you to me forever;*
> *I will betroth you in righteousness and justice,*
> *in love and compassion.*
> *I will betroth you in faithfulness, and you*
> *will acknowledge the Lord.*

Now when someone calls my name, I smile inwardly and feel complete as never before. The Lord has forgiven my unfaithfulness and brought me home. I lack for nothing and remember every day the blessings and security of his steadfast love, even when I least deserve it. Just as God loves his people and keeps his promises, so does my husband remain constant in his devotion.

God promises he will forgive your wickedness and
no longer remember your sins
(Hebrews 8:12).

FOR REFLECTION

"For as high as the heavens are above the earth, so great is his love
for those who fear him; as far as the east is from the west, so far has
he removed our transgressions from us (Psalm 103:11-12).

One of the worst aspects of sin is forgiving yourself. You knew better, but chose to be willful. The consequences left you reeling. Your mind is stuck on the instant replay of punishment.

Here's the deal, though. If you feel remorse, you already have a teachable spirit willing to repent and do better. God will honor tenderness. He knows the temptations you face, and he will rush to your aid when you are ready to repair situations. Spend time thinking about sins you have committed and let those go. Ask God to help you correct the wrongs and set out on the right path.

A PRAYER FOR TODAY

Dear Lord, Please protect me from lust. Help me run to you for
protection from temptation. When I seek the attention of others,
please draw me back to your unconditional love. Keep my eyes on
you to feel desired and special. Amen

Chapter Nine

HOMELESS OPPORTUNITY

$\mathscr{F}$lee. Grab what you can and go. You must leave your home because your life is in danger." Your heart races and perspiration drenches your pajama top. "Pack quickly whatever you can carry. The trip will be long." You sit bolt upright in bed and shake your fuzzy head to clear your thoughts. It's 2:30 a.m. Was what you heard a nightmare or vision?

In a pressing situation where you have to evacuate, what would you grab in a hurry? A small canvas duffel bag would hold a pair of socks and extra underwear. Throw in a full water bottle and a box of raisins, which won't need refrigeration. What else is in the pantry you can take? Add a loaf of bread and a jar of peanut butter? No, the bread would get smooshed, and the jar would be too heavy.

You might need a jacket if it gets cold and bandages if you get blisters walking. What about sunscreen? Suddenly, the commonplace turns into precious items. In frustration, you grit your teeth. There's absolutely no way to include everything you might need. Toothpaste and a toothbrush can fit in the outside pocket, but the large bottle of minty mouthwash stays behind.

Military families have transfers down to an art because they can pack up and move on short notice. They have learned to condense essentials to a pot or two for cooking, bathroom supplies, and sleeping bags. Those in the service know from years of practice whatever they will need at the new duty station will be provided. God frequently issues the same challenge to his people being mobilized for ministry. Defensive and offensive maneuvers require precise logistics if the operation is to succeed. People need resources and protection.

At Christmas time, believers like to share the story of the magi bringing baby Jesus gifts of gold, incense, and myrrh. Woolly sheep look on and brindle cows chew their cuds in contentment. But few study the next verses in Matthew 2 where this extravagant largesse draws dangerous attention to rural Bethlehem. "When they (wise men) had gone, an angel of the Lord appeared to Joseph in a dream. 'Get up,' he said, 'take the child and his mother and escape to Egypt'" (Matthew 2:13).

The angel warned Joseph about the severity of the situation. "Stay there until I tell you, for Herod is going to search for the child to kill him" (Matthew 2:13).

A death threat is a good motivation to run. Joseph didn't roll over and say he'd work on the situation in the morning. He didn't snuggle back under covers and drift off to sleep swearing never again to eat pizza with anchovies. He got up, took the child and his mother *during the night,* and left for Egypt. His obedience was absolute.

King Herod's insane jealousy about a rival royal resulted in an evil decree. Herod directed his soldiers to kill all boys two years old and under around Bethlehem (Matthew 2:16-18). Joseph's diligence spared Jesus from the ensuing bloodbath.

Have you ever had a vivid dream with an important message? Be careful not to discount visions as experiences which only happen in the Bible. Even in modern times, God may interrupt sleep with critical instructions because that is the only time the conscious mind stands down long enough to hear him. God may tap you to pray immediately for someone in danger on the highway. You may pick up the phone and call a lonely person who happened to be considering suicide in the wee hours. God still speaks today in dreams and visions, and the Holy Spirit will guide you how to verify the accuracy of the information you sense.

Joseph heeded the warning in the night and prepared his family for flight. While you might think God's son would be surrounded by servants and palatial elegance, this special little one started in a rustic setting only to become homeless. How unexpected for God's human emissary to have few worldly belongings. Don't you wish you could talk with Joseph how he planned the trip to Egypt?

He certainly couldn't call the American Automobile Association or google directions. There was no cruise control nor air conditioning. He relied on legs, his own and possibly those with hooves, to carry his family many miles south. Trying to cart the treasure chests left by the wise men seemed out of the question for a low-key getaway. Pocketing some coins, Joseph trusted God to provide. There certainly weren't any ATMs.

Their journey from Bethlehem to Egypt is estimated to be about 40 miles, according to a 2017 Egyptian news article where the journey was recreated for tourism.[10] Consider Mary's comfort, or lack thereof. She may have been breastfeeding. No disposable diapers to be had. How cranky did little Jesus get when flies buzzed around his head and there was no quiet room for napping in the afternoon heat? Did his little bottom get diaper rash? Not to mention how hard it must have been for Mary and Joseph to take turns carrying his little behind mile after mile.

People preparing for the U.S. Army's Special Forces Assessment Course often carry a 50-pound ruck sack over rough terrain and trek 18 miles in four and a half hours.[11] In a Military.com post online, Stew Smith advises soldier wannabes to break in boots by

---

10 Ismail Akwei, "Egypt Retraces Journey of Jesus' Family Through Its Country for Tourism," May 31, 2017, https://www.africanews.com/2017/05/31/egypt-retraces-journey-of-jesus-family-through-its-country-for-tourism//#:-:text=The%20Journey,children%20in%20and%20around%20Bethlehem.

11 Stew Smith, "How to Train for Ruck Marches," Military.com, https://www.military.com/military-fitness/army-workouts/training-for-ruck-marches.

taking a shower with them on, then walking around in them for two hours to mold and improve fit.[12] Not sure how well Joseph and Mary's sandals worked on dusty feet, but you can be sure they kept up a smart pace, all the while looking over their shoulders to see if they were being pursued.

What the Bible doesn't say is almost as tantalizing as what scripture clearly describes. Joseph, Mary, and Jesus land in Egypt, but where did they stay? What type of work did Joseph get to pay their way? Where did they live in a foreign land populated by former oppressors? Those questions don't seem to matter in the big picture of following God's will. He knows the future and guides with specific instructions so you will be where you are supposed to be, no matter how unlikely a location in your eyes.

Maybe you have to relocate, and dread the inconvenience and uncertainty—not to mention the cost of uprooting. You feel sad to leave behind family and friends. The question becomes whether you will have welcoming neighbors at the new place, assuming you even get a home to buy. Though change is nerve-racking, God wouldn't have you go without good reason.

His justifications don't always include what seems expedient. However, a mentor may be at the new job site who can help you acquire the leadership skills you will need five years from now as a supervisor. A new friend may leave behind atheism because of your witness. What if you missed that divine appointment and no one else could touch that person's heart? Your children may be protected from a pedophile because God knows the fancy subdivision you covet hides darkness behind closed doors. In the moment when your closing falls through, you don't understand. These deeper insights won't come until *after* you've been obedient.

Transitions stretch you to reassess how you define yourself. Without a nice street address or upscale apartment complex with the pool

---

12 Stew Smith, "How to Train for Ruck Marches," Military.com, https://www.military.com/military-fitness/army-workouts/training-for-ruck-marches.

and lanai, what determines your importance? The trappings of financial success are great to enjoy and often represent God's favor, but he values you even if you live out of a backpack with one tattered T-shirt to your name.

Listen how Jesus cautioned a potential follower not to expect an easy life walking God's path. "Foxes have dens and birds have nests, but the Son of Man has no place to lay his head" (Luke 9:58). If Jesus didn't focus on property holdings, why should you?

Joseph and Mary hid out in Egypt a few years until Herod died. In another dream, an angel told Joseph, "Get up, take the child and his mother and go to the land of Israel, for those who were trying to take the child's life are dead" (Matthew 2:19).

Seriously? Mary may have thought. *I just got the living room arranged like I want and now I have to leave again? There's no way we can take the new dining room furniture we just paid off.* Yet she and her husband made the arduous trek more than 100 miles north to settle in Nazareth (Matthew 2:22-23).[13]

Having a safe, attractive place to live is desirable. But don't be disappointed if God asks you to move. He may test your resolve as He leads you to trails with more spiritual potential. Can you slough off unnecessary attachments to do what he asks?

Rabbi Chaim Weiner explains the word usually translated as "house" or "home," which in Hebrew is *Bayit*.[14] He writes in an online post, "The huge range of meanings of the word shows lots of places can be home; indeed almost anywhere can be home. A home isn't about space; a home is a state of mind."[15]

---

13 Ismail Akwei, "Egypt Retraces Journey of Jesus' Family Through Its Country for Tourism," May 31, 2017, https://www.africanews.com/2017/05/31/egypt-retraces-journey-of-jesus-family-through-its-country-for-tourism//#:~:text=The%20Journey,children%20in%20and%20around%20 Bethlehem.

14 Rabbi Chaim Weiner, "[Bayit] – There Is No Place Like Home," My Hebrew Word by Masorti Europe, Wordpress, https://myhebrewwords.wordpress.com/2015/12/17/19-%D7%91%D7%99%D7%AA-bayit-there-is-no-place-like-home/.

15 Ibid.

Recall in Exodus 16 how God took the Israelites from slavery in Egypt through the dry desert before he deposited them in the land of milk and honey. For most of the trip, they grumbled about not getting the food they wanted. They had no idea of the beautiful vineyards and fruitful fig trees they could own for themselves if they just kept walking in faith. Think like a spiritual investment advisor: Look for opportunities that will pay long-term dividends. Sometimes, God asks you to give something up for a short time to free your hands for receiving the better gift he wants to offer.

If God establishes you in a set territory to manage, be the best steward you can be. Yet if he asks you to go to a new locale or role, don't fear. His final destination is a home for you for eternity. Jesus tells you not to let your heart be troubled. He promises, "My Father's house has many rooms; if it were not so, would I have told you that I am going there to prepare a place for you?" (John 14:2).

There's going to be an awesome party with helium balloons and yellow ribbons wrapped around stately oaks when you have the ultimate family reunion. All the sad goodbyes will become joyous hellos.

***God promises he will provide a home for his people
where the wicked can no longer
oppress them (1 Chronicles 17:9).***

FOR REFLECTION

*"How lovely is your dwelling place, Lord Almighty. My soul yearns,
even faints, for the courts of the Lord; my heart and my flesh cry out
for the living God. Even the sparrow has found a home, and the
swallow a nest for herself, where she may have her young—a place
near your altar, Lord Almighty, my King and my God. Blessed are*

those who dwell in your house; they are ever praising you"
(Psalm 84:1-4).

When you associate identity with the physical structure of your residence, you can get distracted from what God is doing. He may ask you to move out and explore new territory. He may use this change to remind you to depend solely on him.

There is nothing wrong with wanting a nice home and working hard to take care of one. You just don't want those activities to overshadow your focus on God. As birds like sparrows and swallows settle their young in convenient perches, look for the place God wants you to occupy. If a move or job change is imminent, will you trust him during the change?

A PRAYER FOR TODAY

Dear Lord, I can get stuck in one spot and not want to go where you want to take me. I fear new places and cling to what's familiar. Please help me trust you more. My home is with you, and the physical scenery doesn't matter when you hold my hand. Together, we will face whatever is ahead. Amen

Chapter Ten

LOCKED LIP SYNC

$\mathcal{W}$hen you think of power, what comes to mind? Some might say making national decisions, having vast financial wealth, leading huge armies, or wielding great physical strength. But how about the power of words to destroy or heal?

Consider the difference between these two phrases: "You are fat." and "You are phat." The first expression might imply a person is overweight and undesirable, but the second can be slang for highly attractive. What a difference spelling makes. In English, there are more than 171,000 words in use, according to the Oxford English Dictionary.[16] How many of these do you use in a positive fashion daily? People yearn for affirmation in an era when criticism dominates.

Proverbs 12:14 says: "From the fruit of their lips people are filled with good things, and the work of their hands brings them reward." A boss praising your efforts finalizing a new deal makes you redouble efforts to help the company grow. An instructor who compliments your assignment encourages you to research the topic more. A parent who commends you for organizing the family get-together increases your willingness to host again. A friend shares how much you mean to him and how he counts on your advice.

---

16 Beth Sagar-Fenton and Lizzy McNeill, "How Many Words Do You Need to Speak a Language?" More or Less, BBC Radio 4, 24 June 2018, at https://www.bbc.com/news/world-44569277#:~:text=We%20considered%20dusting%20off%20the,to%20mention%2047%2C156%20obsolete%20words.

These examples of words being used to build up people show the influence of language on lives.

Try tracking a mental log how you deploy words today. Keep in mind: "The words of the reckless pierce like a sword, but the tongue of the wise brings healing" (Proverbs 12:18). Slow down and process what you are saying before you spew something you may regret later. Ask yourself if what you are about to say is necessary. "The prudent keep their knowledge to themselves, but a fool's heart blurts out folly" (Proverbs 12:23).

Listening is becoming a lost art. People are quick to spout an opinion and miss an opportunity to hear another perspective. "The way of fools seems right to them, but the wise listen to advice" (Proverbs 12:15). King Solomon, touted as a great ruler who built a vast kingdom in the early 900s B.C., compiled much of Proverbs to guide his sons.[17] Some 2,000 years later, the advice holds true. If you are pressed for time, but want to gain insights in better ways to live, reading a proverb or two a day can reap great results tuning into a godly perspective.

The alternative is 'doomscrolling,' which is a recent term for the tendency to skim news and focus on the negatives.[18] This would be when you get a raise and complain the percentage is too low compared to other job sectors. Another example would be when new vaccines are released, but people gripe lines for shots are too long. The entire focus is on negativity, and no ounce of optimism is allowed. That's not how God wants us to live.

The fourth book of the New Testament was written around 90 A.D. by John, one of Jesus' closest followers and friends.[19] Here's how he prioritized content: "In the beginning was the Word, and the

---

17 Timeline Index, "Solomon, 3rd King of Israel," https://www.timelineindex.com/content/view/2714.

18 Korin Miller, "What is Doomscrolling? Experts Explain Why We Do It—and How to Stop," Health.com, June 17, 2020 at https://www.health.com/mind-body/what-is-doomscrolling.

19 Marilyn Mellowes, "An Introduction to the Gospels," Frontline: From Jesus to Christ, April 1998, https://www.pbs.org/wgbh/pages/frontline/shows/religion/story/mmfour.html#:~:text=The%20Gospel%20of%20John%2C%20sometimes,Jesus%20in%20a%20different%20way.

Word was with God, and the Word was God" (John 1:1). What an interesting focus on "Word."

John saw Jesus change water into wine (John 2) and heal an invalid who hadn't walked in 38 years (John 5). This disciple saw Jesus fed 5,000 people with a few loaves of bread (John 6) and raise Lazarus from the dead (John 11). He also witnessed Jesus appearing in a resurrected body after public execution (John 20). Any of these events summarized Jesus' amazing capacities. Why then did John lead with "word" instead of "miracle?"

Perhaps John realized ordinary followers had the same power as Jesus, if they used the words he taught them. The next two sentences of John's introduction include: "He was with God in the beginning. Through him all things were made; without him nothing was made" (John 1:2-3). Before a model can be constructed, an idea has to occur. New symbols or words develop to represent the budding concept. Words spotlight creations and draw attention to the potential.

At the inception of the world, God "formed out of the ground all the wild animals and all the birds in the sky" (Genesis 2:19). Then God did a surprising thing. Instead of labeling each creation, he invited Adam to name them. "Whatever the man called each living creature, that was its name"(Genesis 2:19). There is incredible authority in the words you speak. Think of the care that goes into naming a child. A tone and identity are set that shape a life.

Names can connote the continuation of a distinguished family line, such as with Elizabeth II. There also can be playful originality signaling a departure from tradition. A Mom Junction online article tracked popular and funny baby names for 2020. The number nine nomination was "Fifi Trixibelle" for the daughter of Irish singer Bob Geldof. Reportedly, "Fifi" honors his aunt. "Belle" represents his wife's love of French belles. The "Trixi" part was a surprise.[20] Taking

---

20 Bhavana Navuluri, "100 Most Popular and Funny Baby Names of 2020 Revealed," Mom Junction, December 9, 2020, https://www.momjunction.com/articles/funny-baby-names_00342523/.

place at number 36 was "Mustard M. Mustard."[21] No telling what effect that repetition might have. Maybe the parents loved seasoning food. Or perhaps the pregnant mom preferred sauce to pickles. Either way, the child will have an easy time learning to write his full name.

You have the power to speak into existence what sort of attitude you want. Upbeat outlooks bring joy. "In him was life, and that life was the light of men," John added. "The light shines in the darkness, and the darkness has not overcome it" (John 1:4-5). In a time filled with cares and burdens, use words that bring hope and encouragement.

Exercise your God-given power to create phrases that bring healing. "Hygge" is a new term that means making a person feel comfortable.[22] Whom can you compliment today? How can you show hospitality and welcome others into your home, workplace, or neighborhood? Being a grouch surely won't bring God any seekers.

Pretend you are at a lip sync battle representing Jesus against the forces of darkness. How can you perform his music and lyrics to spotlight glory? Study his stage presence and mimic his affirmations to bring the audience to its feet. Rock the beat and bring the party. Let them applaud his love.

Be in sync with Philippians 4:8: "Whatever is true, whatever is noble, whatever is right, whatever is pure, whatever is lovely, whatever is admirable—if anything is excellent or praiseworthy—think about such things." Paul ended that passage asking the followers of Jesus to put into practice all they had learned or heard. "And the God of peace will be with you" (Philippians 4:9).

God promises he will give you the right words to say to accomplish his work (John 14:10).

---

21 Bhavana Navuluri, "100 Most Popular and Funny Baby Names of 2020 Revealed," Mom Junction, December 9, 2020, https://www.momjunction.com/articles/funny-baby-names_00342523/.

22 Merriam-Webster.com, "We Added New Words to the Dictionary," January 2021, https://www.merriam-webster.com/words-at-play/new-words-in-the-dictionary.

FOR REFLECTION

"Do not let any unwholesome talk come out of your mouths, but only what is helpful for building others up according to their needs, that it may benefit those who listen" (Ephesians 4:29).

Consider someone who uses words wisely. How does that person phrase statements so others can receive the information?

Now, think about someone who offends others by what they say, even if the intent was good. How can you learn from that awkward example to ensure you don't make the same mistake?

Little ears (and big ones, too) always are listening. What phrases and tone of voice do you hear in your children? They are parroting you. Try a new game at work or with your family. Clean out a pickle jar and cut a coin-size slot in the cap. Every time someone says an uplifting word, put a coin in the jar. When full, buy a gallon of ice cream for all to share in the sweetness of the spoken word.

A PRAYER FOR TODAY

Dear Lord, I want the words from my mouth to bring life and hope. Please help me develop the discipline to spend time in the Bible to add to my vocabulary of love. When people leave a conversation with me, I want them to feel joy, not discouragement. Please show me how. Amen

Chapter Eleven

BOUNTIFUL BLUE HARVEST

*W*hile words form beliefs, actions determine physical results. You can dream all day about having certain things in life, but if you don't start working, nothing happens. God doesn't want you reclining on the sofa surfing channels, gorging on junk food, and turning into a couch potato. Look at nature to understand how effort is required. "Go to the ant, you sluggard; consider its ways and be wise. It has no commander, no overseer or ruler, yet it stores its provisions in summer and gathers its food at harvest" (Proverbs 6:6-8).

Ants do not seek acclaim. They perform for the good of the colony, which could number in the thousands. Each has a role to play. Workers may clean the eggs, tend larvae, or forage for food.[23] None will sit idle or fail to contribute. However, humans often dodge responsibility.

Too often, you want God to be a cosmic genie who grants wishes whenever you want. In this modern society with instant gratification, many have lost the concept of planting dreams with daily efforts and waiting for them to come to fruition. Farmers and gardeners have an advantage knowing the rules of sowing before reaping.

---

23 Western Exterminator Company, "The Ant Colony: Structure and Roles," https://www.westernexterminator.com/ants/the-ant-colony-structure-and-roles/.

Blueberry bushes with emerald leaves can take a year to generate their delicious crop. Before you can pop sweet fruit into your mouth, plants must be fertilized and weeded. Insects must be kept away. Mites can attack the buds, and blight can destroy a stem. There's no guarantee the produce will mature. There may be too much rain or not enough. A cold snap may ruin the blossoms. Acidic soil is preferred and bees help pollinate.

What starts as a simple venture requires dedication and education. You can talk all day about how much you love eating blueberries, but until you commit to the process and see it through, you will take much for granted. Those neat plastic containers in the grocery store don't tell the whole story.

To be a healthy Christian, you need to be productive. "What good is it, my brothers and sisters, if someone claims to have faith but has no deeds?" (James 2:14). You know Jesus' sacrifice saves you, but that doesn't mean camp out with religious elite and toast s'mores over the fire. Jesus equips you to serve. He invests unique talents and life experiences so you can bring good food to the hungry.

"They sowed fields and planted vineyards that yielded a fruitful harvest; he blessed them, and their numbers greatly increased, and he did not let their herds diminish" (Psalm 107:37). Are you willing to put your hands in soil and have sweat trickle down your back to co-labor in worthy projects? Or do you want to stay in the fast food drive-through line and find convenient ways to meet your needs? You might even beep that horn to hurry everyone along, so you'll get to the window faster. But taking shortcuts doesn't bring God's praise.

The disciple Paul has strong words in the New Testament for believers who say "religious" phrases but don't act on the godly principles. "A man reaps what he sows. Whoever sows to please their flesh, from the flesh will reap destruction; whoever sows to please the Spirit, from the Spirit will reap eternal life" (Galatians 6:7-8).

Small habits matter. Do you read gory novels or uplifting books? Late at night, do you watch sketchy movies you wouldn't want your children to walk in on? At the office, do you take unauthorized breaks to check your cell phone messages? While these choices in and of themselves may not be horrendous, they can establish a pattern undermining overall performance.

People watch what Christians do. They measure whether the daily walk enforces the "talk." A believer who calls out frequently at the last minute from a shift and leaves co-workers short-handed or who often arrives tardy isn't a good witness. If a person isn't reliable in daily chores, how can he or she be trusted for complex spiritual guidance? Others need to see believers are consistently living out honorable principles.

People notice those who do extra without complaint. In the Old Testament, young Ruth volunteered to work in the fields to get food for herself and mother-in-law. Because of the tragic deaths of their husbands, the women had no means of support. Ruth had a can-do mindset. She looked for options instead of excuses.

In a quiet, efficient manner, she politely asked the foreman if she may line up behind the harvesters and gather any sheaves left behind. Harvesters moved in a clockwise circle. Some would cut the stalks. Others tied up the bunches, then stacked sheaves for the grain heads to dry.[24] With humility, Ruth joined the team. She kept pace and observed their process, so she didn't get in their way. Maybe she looked for places to help and offered a few stalks of grain to a nearby girl struggling to keep up.

Ruth worked under the hot sun without slacking. She didn't impose on anyone, nor did she play the victim recounting the hard life she'd had. She earned respect from other laborers with her consistent effort. When Boaz, who owned the field, arrived he noticed the new girl and asked the foreman about her.

The supervisor gave a good report. "She came into the field and has remained here from morning till now, except for a short rest in the

---

24 LEO Design, Ltd., "Barley Sheaves," https://leodesignnyc.com/blogs/journal/unfinished-1-13-19.

shelter" (Ruth 2:7). Anyone who has been employed in agriculture understands the grueling nature of bending and walking hours on end. The sun beats down and muscles complain, but there lies ahead row after row yet to do.

Ruth didn't falter. She didn't find an easy way out. She may have hummed a tune from her homeland to pass the time. Maybe she smiled at a girl near her swatting a fly. Ruth knew the temporary discomfort brought a huge reward: being able to provide for her beloved mother-in-law. Imagining Naomi's pride kept Ruth going even when she wanted to quit.

Her selfless reputation gained notice. Boaz approached her and told her to stay in his fields where she would be safe. He told her to drink water from the jars his men had filled. At this unexpected generosity, Ruth bowed down with her face to the ground. This gratitude is not something you see these days. She exclaimed, "Why have I found such favor in your eyes that you notice me—a foreigner?" (Ruth 2:10). Her appreciation for Boaz's kindness made him want to do even more for her.

How often do you remember to thank others for their service? When a person allows you to go first in line, do you acknowledge the courtesy? Too often, people focus on what they want and don't see a need right in front of their face. If you are in a grocery store and observe a person in a scooter straining to reach a high shelf, what do you do? How easy for you to say "hello" and pass down the box or jar. Circling in a busy parking lot? Wave that senior citizen in the approaching vehicle into the prime spot. There'll be another for you around the corner.

Ruth found favor precisely because she didn't expect it. Boaz offered to share the meal of bread dipped in vinegar. Was she so poor she didn't have a lunch to bring? She must have been worried sick about how Naomi fared back at home. Boaz passed along the serving dish piled high with roasted grain and told her to take as much as she wanted. He did this casually to protect her pride.

He watched her carefully wrap up what was left of her picnic. Boaz suspected she would take the snacks back for Naomi's dinner, and he was right. The workers appreciated his thoughtfulness, and their families fared well because of his caring.

Notice that Boaz stay involved. He didn't hang back in the air-conditioned C-suite with his feet propped up on a mahogany desk admiring his Rolex until time to golf. This manager knew his workers personally and walked the job site with them. As supervisor, he ensured their protection and well-being with adequate food, water, and a shelter for shade from the punishing sun. This management style honored the people and encouraged them to give their best.

Ruth gleaned in the field until evening, but she didn't stop there. She took the extra step of separating the grain heads from the stalks, so she wouldn't have so much to carry back after a long day. Her threshing efforts measured close to one bushel.[25] This amount in wheat grain could bake into as many as "90 one-pound loaves of whole wheat bread" according to the National Association of Wheat Growers.[26]

Though her shoulders ached and her nose was sunburned, Ruth probably smiled to think about Naomi's reaction when she finally got home to show the day's earnings. Ruth could almost smell the fragrance of cooked barley bread drizzled with honey that Naomi could make.[27] Ruth's mouth watered. She felt reassured they would find a way forward and prosper. With such abundance, maybe they could trade for new sandals and dried figs.

Because she was willing to work, Ruth's future brightened. She not only reaped the harvest of grain, but she also ended up marrying a godly man. Boaz proposed to her because of her noble character and great loyalty. Ruth accepted Boaz's marriage proposal, knowing him

---

25 Benson Commentary, Bible Hub, "Ruth 2:17," https://biblehub.com/commentaries/ruth/2-17.htm.

26 National Association of Wheat Growers, "Wheat Facts," https://www.wheatworld.org/wheat-101/wheat-facts/#:~:text=A%20bushel%20of%20wheat%20yields,half%20pound%20loaf%20of%20bread.

27 Chocolatl Recipe, Egpytian Barley Bread, https://www.food.com/recipe/egyptian-barley-bread-423725.

to be an astute businessman who was generous and kind. Together, they parented their son, Obed, who became part of David's genealogy, as well as Jesus' (Ruth 4:13-22). Because Ruth and Boaz had positive attitudes and invested effort, God expanded their territory. He will do the same for you as you prove yourself a reliable steward.

> *God promises he will establish his everlasting covenant not only with you, but also with your descendants for generations to come*
> *(Genesis 17:7).*

FOR REFLECTION

"Let us not become weary in doing good, for at the proper time we will reap a harvest if we do not give up" (Galatians: 6:9).

Though poor, Ruth worked hard. This positioned her for success. She wasn't too proud to do a lowly job picking up leftover grain in barley fields (Ruth 2:1-2). She may not have had much, but her back was strong and she intended to use it.

Ask people in your social circle to help you identify your strengths. Tell them you are inventorying assets to move forward in tough times. What do they notice about you they admire? At the next team meeting or family dinner night, ask each person to write at least one admirable trait they see in someone else. These cards can be shared and kept for encouragement.

A PRAYER FOR TODAY

Dear Lord, Sometimes, I get lazy and don't want to do what I know is the right thing. Unlike Ruth, I don't particularly want to labor in a hot field doing a thankless job. However, if I adjust my attitude, I will reap many rewards. Please help me have a willing heart, trusting you will provide as I step out to complete today's work. Amen

Chapter Twelve

SHAKE YOUR BOOTY

$\mathcal{M}$ist veils the early morning ground like dry ice rising above a stage. Two sand-hill cranes dance in an open field near the oak tree. They whirl, looking elegant with long necks extended. In silent stilted steps, they bow toward each other, then dip with funny little pirouettes. These birds stand about four feet tall and have a wingspan close to five feet.[28] Scarlet scarves adorn their heads, and dark stockings cover slender legs. Blue-gray tuxedoes with golden threads on the chest complete their attire.

Silvery wings flair out at their midriff as though they are putting hands on hips in an Elizabethan ballroom. These creatures circle each other with formality, barely touching wingtips like the upper-class men and women in a courtly paval of the 1500s.[29] Then the tempo changes and accelerates. The tall birds add in a hop-skip-leap straight from street pop culture to complete the choreography. Sandhill cranes mate for life, and they can live 20 years.[30] Though their dancing is usually courtship behavior, they can boogie all year. With no self-consciousness, the couple spins around to music of its own.

---

28 The National Wildlife Federation, "Sandhill Crane," https://www.nwf.org/Educational-Resources/Wildlife-Guide/Birds/Sandhill-Crane.

29 Dance Facts, "Elizabethan Dance and Dancers," http://www.dancefacts.net/dance-history/elizabethan-dance/.

30 The National Wildlife Federation, "Sandhill Crane," https://www.nwf.org/Educational-Resources/Wildlife-Guide/Birds/Sandhill-Crane.

Dancing celebrates strong feelings words alone are inadequate to express. The pastime dates to ancient customs, though styles have changed. If you feel happy, you might execute a jig as did the people of Israel after God delivered them from enemies. With God's favor comes the freedom to move around in comfort and safety. He assures his obedient: "I have drawn you with unfailing kindness. I will build you up ... Again you will take up your timbrels and go out to dance with the joyful" (Jeremiah 31:3-4).

When was the last time you danced? Not just at a party or with a date, but with God?

He created sound waves and instruments to play. Our Creator designed your amazing body to tap toes and hum. The Lord likes seeing you dance for him. You might do a Carolina swing in the garage because you got good news. Consider shuffling a jazz routine when a loved one leaves the hospital for a full recovery. Tango at midnight because the moon is full. Ask him to join you. Not many people do.

They pray for blessings. Seek protection. Petition on behalf of loved ones who have lost their way. But few people understand God likes to hold you close and two-step. No agenda. No demands. Just being together fills his heart. He will be delighted at your invitation.

You will find it doesn't matter what's going on outside his embrace. The music creates a cocoon where all you can see is him looking at you with love. While he leads you step by step with his hand holding yours, following is simple. His footing is sure and his hold on you is secure.

When the Israelites were going through hardships, the prophet Jeremiah encouraged them to hang on and know good times were ahead. Problems would be overcome. "Then young women will dance and be glad, young men and old as well. I will turn their mourning into gladness; I will give them comfort and joy instead of sorrow" (Jeremiah 31:13).

As your dance partner, God counts off the steps of your life one-and-two, three-and-four. He moves around the ballroom of experiences and turns you in new directions. Relax in his arms. He knows the way. His fancy footwork in glossy black dress shoes will take you on a breathless circuit that keeps you feeling alive and loved. Around and around you may go, till you feel quite dizzy, then he switches counterclockwise and heaven applauds the adroit turn. Dance into your destiny.

God is full of surprising moves. If he sees someone stepping on your toes, he will intervene. "I have indeed seen the misery of my people in Egypt. I have heard them crying out because of their slave drivers, and I am concerned about their suffering. So I have come down to rescue them ...." (Exodus 3:7-8). He sent Moses to fetch the Israelites from the pharaoh. Timidly, Moses agreed to speak God's commands to the foreign king. However, royalty wasn't excited to free their laborers.

Moses' knees shook as he asked for permission for them to leave. Pharaoh's face purpled with rage. God scheduled demonstrations to prove to the Egyptian ruler he wasn't playing around. The Lord changed the Nile's water into blood and made it undrinkable (Exodus 7). He assigned frogs to march on the city and fill up houses (Exodus 8). He dispatched gnats and flies to swarm and make the captors miserable (Exodus 8), then Egyptian livestock succumbed to a plague (Exodus 9).

How stubborn Pharaoh must have been. Yet, we behave the same way when God closes doors and asks for patient obedience. We refuse. Maybe you ignored God's warnings about consequences for going your own way.

Apparently, Pharaoh didn't catch on quickly. So, God also sent boils to fester on Egyptians' skin, hail to destroy livestock, and locusts to devour crops and trees. Pharaoh would relent for a short time to stop the disasters, then renege on allowing all the Israelite families to leave with their belongings to worship the Lord.

Total darkness covered the land for three days while Pharaoh stewed how to keep his slaves without his country enduring any more punishment. Finally, God decreed every firstborn, whether human or animal, would die in the night. The only protection came for those who painted the sacrificial blood of a pure lamb on the doorframe of their home (Exodus 12:21-23).

Pause for a moment and absorb how this Old Testament ritual foreshadowed what Jesus would do for you. He willingly gave up every privilege to ensure you would be with him in his kingdom. Your Savior will let no force deprive him of your company. This heavenly champion will let no other isolate you from him.

God gave Pharaoh chance after chance, but only at midnight when all the Egyptian firstborn died, did Pharaoh at last dismiss Moses and his people. Amid the wailing of bereaved Egyptians, their slaves took the God-given escape. "The Israelites journeyed from Rameses to Sukkoth. There were about six hundred thousand men on foot, besides women and children" (Exodus 12:37). This teeming mass of civilians must have been shell-shocked to leave the place where a seemingly invincible oppressor had held them captive for more than 400 years.

Have you waited a long time for God to move in your life? Have you wondered if he really exists? He is alive and well. His silence doesn't mean he isn't watching. Maybe he wants to see if you are ready to move out and leave your place of captivity. Consider what fears you have allowed to imprison you in an unhealthy place.

Even when you decide you want a better life and don't want to be trapped, don't be surprised if there are many obstacles to hold you back. You jump one hurdle, only to stumble on a rock and bruise your foot. Pharaohs enjoy destroying your confidence and intimidating you into thinking there is no way out. But keep moving. God will deliver.

Just as the Israelites relaxed, enjoying the new scenery with the fresh scent of freedom, bam. They hear the unmistakable thud of galloping horses. They see hundreds of chariots careening toward them. Women glanced nervously toward tired children as the men tried to keep the skittish livestock under control. They had nowhere to run. The former slaves panicked, but Moses didn't. "Do not be afraid. Stand firm and you will see the deliverance the Lord will bring you today. The Lord will fight for you; you need only to be still" (Exodus 14:13-14).

The next part of the story may give you goosebumps. "Then the angel of God, who had been traveling in front of Israel's army, withdrew and went behind them. The pillar of cloud also moved from in front and stood behind them, coming between the armies of Egypt and Israel" (Exodus 14:19-20). You may not see how God positions his heavenly forces, but they stand at attention and execute his commands without hesitation. They protect you too.

With the Egyptians in hot pursuit, the Israelites have their backs pinned against the sea. Escape looks impossible. However, throughout the tense night, God marshalled a strong east wind to turn the water away and carve out dry land for the Israelites to pass. With rising walls of water on either side, they traveled in the supernatural corridor till the last watch of the night. Not to be daunted, pharaoh and his fighters followed into the sea. Then God made the wheels of their chariots fall off, resulting in collisions and chaos (Exodus 14:21-25).

At daybreak when all the Israelites were safely on the other side, God told Moses to stretch out his hand and release the sea back to its natural state. The brave Israelite men who volunteered to be the rear guard felt their knees weaken as the chariots charged toward them, closer and closer. The enemy was so near the Israelites probably could see the horses' mouths flecked with foam from the headlong chase.

Then the pursuers became the hunted. The Egyptians may have screamed in terror as the wall of braced water crashed down. After the roar of furious waves capsizing chariots, then there was silence. Maybe an Egyptian helmet or boot floated on the surface, but that was all. "Not one of them survived" (Exodus 14:28).

The Israelites must have stood in awe at the devastation God had wreaked on their pursuers. "And when the Israelites saw the mighty hand of the Lord displayed against the Egyptians, the people feared the Lord and put their trust in him and in Moses his servant" (Exodus 14:31).

While you may want to avoid conflict, difficulties may be what absolutely convinces you God is real and he is working on your behalf. Others who witness the deliverance you enjoy also will put their confidence in a God capable of miracles.

In the moments of victory, that's when the party starts. Moses and the Israelites began singing and praising God. Do you? When you look at a sunrise or witness a thunderstorm, do you see his handiwork? If so, kick up your heels and do the Charleston. "Who among the gods is like you, Lord? Who is like you—majestic in holiness, awesome in glory, working wonders?" (Exodus 15:11). God appreciates whole-hearted yodeling more than a tepid sing-along. He is worthy.

Don't be shy. Miriam wasn't. As soon as she realized how God had protected her people, when moments before defeat seemed imminent, she grabbed a tambourine and started dancing. She clapped the heel of her hand to the stretched skin and rattled jangles. Her lithe figure skipped forward with her earrings sparkling in the light and her bracelets jingling in rhythm. And in a moment of complete abandon, she even may have shaken her robed rear as she shouted, "Sing to the Lord, for he is highly exalted. Both horse and driver he has hurled into the sea" (Exodus 15:21).

You too can dance in joy because God is present in your life. Doesn't matter if it's Irish clogging or ballet turns. God will waltz right along with you. You are his favorite partner.

God promises he will turn your sorrow into gladness, and he will provide comfort and joy (Jeremiah 31:13).

FOR REFLECTION

"You turned my wailing into dancing; you removed my sackcloth and clothed me with joy, that my heart may sing your praises and not be silent" (Psalm 30:11-12).

"But may the righteous be glad and rejoice before God; may they be happy and joyful. Sing to God, sing in praise of his name, extol him who rides on the clouds; rejoice before him—his name is the Lord" (Psalm 68:3-4).

"Let the message of Christ dwell among you richly as you teach and admonish one another with all wisdom through psalms, hymns, and songs from the Spirit, singing to God with gratitude in your hearts" (Colossians 3:16).

When was a time you were happy? How did knowledge of God's presence enrich that moment? Sometimes, you get so busy working or "being spiritual" that spontaneity and joy are lost. Interrupt the being-so-responsible routine.

Go put on music you like that gets your toes tapping. Imagine God beside you clapping his hands to the beat. Accept his offer of carefree companionship and enjoy lightheartedness. Let your weary soul sing.

A PRAYER FOR TODAY

Dear Lord, Life can be full of sorrow and trouble. Those "Egyptians" of fear, worry, and doubt are in hot pursuit. My peace of mind depends on your love for me. Just as you divinely saved the Israelites, please help me see the miracles you are doing on my behalf right now. Even in the middle of a mess, help me dance with joy because you are with me. Hold me close and let me hear the song you play for just the two of us. Amen

Chapter Thirteen

GPS: GOD'S PERSONAL SATELLITE

A soothing voice provides directions as you navigate a busy highway. "Four hundred feet ahead, bear right." Isn't it reassuring to have guidance? "Stay in the center lane." The dashboard diagram maps out which lane to choose to prepare for turns and specifies how far to travel before the next move. Gone are the days when you had to squint at tiny symbols on folded paper. With convenient global positioning through satellites, you wonder how you got around before.

Thirty-one satellites in medium earth orbit provide users with accurate location within 25 feet about 95% of the time.[31] Imagine 100 percent accuracy from any distance. This is true when you rely on the Holy Spirit to provide specific instructions for life. Just as the floating man-made structures monitor locations, so does God invite his people to tune into his transmissions for advice.

No expensive updates are needed, nor do you have to worry about signals failing. You only have to turn the knob of your heart to hear. Yet that reliance is counter-culture, particularly in the United States, where independence is prized. You may have thought, *I can do this*

---

31 Federal Aviation Administration, "Satellite Navigation – GPS- How It Works," July 22, 2020, https://www.faa.gov/about/office_org/headquarters_offices/ato/service_units/techops/navservices/ gnss/gps/howitworks/#:~:text=GPS%20satellites%20carry%20atomic%20clocks,time%20 the%20signal%20was%20broadcast.&text=Thus%2C%20the%20receiver%20uses%20four- ,longitude%2C%20altitude%2C%20and%20time.

by myself. Well, there is a hard way to do things—and a smart one. Why barrel ahead into the unknown when you can pause a moment to ensure you are on a safe trajectory? With a little planning, you can avoid collisions and costly detours.

You trust a plastic handheld device to pinpoint travel without being able to understand how satellites and ground stations track you, yet the system works. The equipment constantly sends and listens for signals.[32] God tries to do the same with you. Are you willing to pause and receive his messages?

Global Positioning Systems (GPS) operate with three components: satellites, ground stations, and receivers.[33] Think of God as the satellite in the heavens tracking overall patterns, Jesus as the ground station receiving God's input, and the Holy Spirit as the receiver who makes data connections. They work together to communicate with you, if you choose to listen. Why do you depend on mobile devices more readily than the One who assembled the galaxies where the satellites orbit?

Sometimes, questioning the "Why?" of everything just gives you a headache. You can't connect the dots on your own, and God isn't under any obligation to reveal the entirety of his plan. Besides, when he does, people often ignore the counsel offered. In the New Testament, a disciple named Stephen tried to tell people God's message, but he faced opposition.

Stephen resided in Jerusalem. He, a man full of God's grace and power, did many miracles (Acts 6:8). Jews of Cyrene, Alexandria, and Asia argued with Stephen about what was the truth, "But they could not stand up against the wisdom the Spirit gave him as he spoke" (Acts 6:9).

Despite Stephen's good deeds feeding widows, these hardline Jews wanted to silence his divergent perspective. They set him up on false charges of blasphemy. Stuck in Mosaic tradition, they missed the very

---

32 NASA Science, "How Does GPS Work?" June 27, 2019, https://spaceplace.nasa.gov/gps/en/.
33 Ibid.

prophecy of salvation being fulfilled through Jesus. In their bloodlust to be right, the conspirators lined up false witnesses and railroaded Stephen into court. On trial before the Sanhedrin, the supreme Jewish tribunal for offenses, Stephen spoke eloquently of the history of his people from Abraham to Moses. He hoped to save his audience, but they only desired his demise.

He didn't mince words, telling the crowd surrounding him like a pack of slavering wolves: "You stiff-necked people! Your hearts and ears still are uncircumcised. You are just like your ancestors: You always resist the Holy Spirit! Was there ever a prophet your ancestors did not persecute? They even killed those who predicted the coming of the Righteous One" (Acts 7:51-52).

You can be so convinced you are right following rules, you miss God's surprise turn. His goal isn't to establish an elite club mocking others as inferior. God's goal is to bring all safely to his loving home.

Stephen chastised the Jews staring at him and reminded them they had crucified Jesus. "And now you have betrayed and murdered him—you who have received the law that was given through angels but have not obeyed it" (Acts 7:52-53). Their rich heritage of God's favor as his chosen people tarnished their ability to see God at work in a new way.

Enraged by Stephen's audacity, the crowd yelled at the top of their voices and surrounded him. They dragged him out of the city where they stoned him to death, rock by gory rock. With violence erupting, other followers of Jesus fled to Judea and Samaria. You might think that God messed up the GPS, but the tragedy ultimately resulted in the expansion of preaching to Gentiles, those with no claim to the Jewish heritage. God's plan was much bigger than Jerusalem.

He dispatched a colleague of Stephen's, Philip, to Samaria where ministry resulted in more miracles and changed lives. Unlike what happened in Jerusalem, when the crowds saw what Philip did, "They all paid close attention to what he said" (Acts 8:6). God will not waste words on hard-headed people. He will make every opportunity to share his love and commands, but if people ignore him, he will seek others who are receptive to his message.

Philip must have been joyful to have a warm Samaritan reception after seeing the cruelty in Jerusalem. Maybe Philip hoped he could settle down and establish roots. However, God's GPS pinged on different coordinates. He sent an angel to tell Philip, "Go south to the road—the desert road—that goes down from Jerusalem to Gaza" (Acts 8:26).

One commentary in Bible Gateway translates the passage to mean Philip was to travel at noon, the hottest time of the day, toward the Judean wilderness.[34] Philip didn't argue or call the internet provider to complain the latest updates were faulty. He started out and had a "chance" meeting with an important foreign official traveling the same route. The men struck up a conversation about religion, and Philip shed light on material the official had been reading. The Ethiopian invited Philip to ride in the chariot with him to explain more how a chapter in Isaiah foretold of Jesus' sacrifice for all people. Because Philip yielded to God's mapping, the good news advanced many miles from the Middle East into Africa.

Have you had a similar encounter where God aligned connections just so? A random visit to a new grocery store with a special sale guided you to a reunion with a high school acquaintance taking chemo treatments. A flat tire landed you in a remote repair shop where the owner needed your prayers. You injure your hand playing baseball, only to wait in the hospital's emergency room next to a person hungry for news of God.

These sovereign encounters may be chalked up to chance, but they are part of a divine infrastructure where God designates ministry to occur. He sets you on the proper heading. Allow the Holy Spirit to be your compass daily through Bible readings and prayer. God's magnetic pull draws you to the landmark where lives will be touched.

---

34 Bible Gateway, "Philip and the Ethiopian Eunuch," March 23, 2021 https://www.biblegateway.com/resources/commentaries/IVP-NT/Acts/Philip-Ethiopian-Eunuch.

The worldly GPS navigation system deploys satellites weighing close to 3,000 pounds that cover 12,000-mile rotations twice daily.[35] If human scientists with finite minds can launch such complex equipment, how much more can an omnipotent God do? God does his most remarkable work through believers on the ground attuned to his frequency.

God promises whether you turn to the right or to the left, your ears will hear a voice behind you saying, "This is the way; walk in it" (Isaiah 30:21).

FOR REFLECTION

Jesus told his disciples, "But the Advocate, the Holy Spirit, whom the Father will send in my name, will teach you all things and will remind you of everything I have said to you" (John: 14:26).

God knows many perplexing situations will arise, and you will need help navigating. He communicates with each person in unique ways to guide decisions. Spending time in his Word helps you map out what is the right way to proceed. Studying his truths provides a compass when you travel a new road. With all the technology today, what electronics do you rely upon though you may not explain how they work?

How does the Holy Spirit communicate with you? Can you think of special occasions when you "knew" information originating from a source was beyond your means? The Holy Spirit has your best interests at heart. How can you invite him to help you study the Bible and expand your conversations with him?

35 Marshall Brain and Tom Harris, "How GPS Receivers Work," How Stuff Works: Electronics, https://electronics.howstuffworks.com/gadgets/travel/gps.htm.

A PRAYER FOR TODAY

Dear Lord, I want to hear your directions and follow them. Help me tune into your will, so I don't miss an opportunity. I ask for your guidance to navigate the craziness around me. Please keep me on a true course that honors you. Amen

Chapter Fourteen

AN ALLIGATOR ON THE SIDEWALK

A five-foot-long alligator sauntered along the sidewalk in the midday sun. The reptile, looking as though it were the mayor in a grey suit running for re-election, propelled forward on webbed feet with sharp toenails. Its bumpy tail extended onto the tended lawn. Gators have a place in the ecosystem, but that does not include parading around in a subdivision in broad daylight where innocents push baby strollers and walk their small dogs.

Alligators resemble Satan's stooges: they usually sneak around at night and camouflage under water with only their periscope eyes showing. But with time, if alligators aren't checked, they act with increasing boldness, putting others at risk. Gators have sharp sight and stay on the lookout for easy prey.[36] As an analogy, this would be naïve people visiting murky places where they don't see risks at hand.

One example would be when a person goes to a psychic for a reading. Instead of trusting God for answers, the person gets impatient, or is ill-advised, and tampers with secret and dangerous things. Occult practices are forbidden for God's people. No one may "practice divination or sorcery, interpret omens, engage in witchcraft, or cast spells,

---

36 Everglades Holiday Park, "What Time Do Alligators Feed the Most?" https://www.evergladesholidaypark.com/when-do-alligators-feed/.

or be a medium or spiritist who consult the dead" (Deuteronomy 18:10-11).

Sadly, these pagan practices continue. Even in today's ultramodern and technologically savvy era, people tread in realms inhabited by reptiles. Look online and you will see many ads for Tarot cards, crystal ball readings, and spells to "help" find "answers and love." According to a 2021 professional companies directory, a psychic session for an individual costs from $30 to $100.[37] There is no altruistic motive—just greed. The tricksters pounce on those who ignore the safe boundary God establishes. God's wisdom is free. He only asks us to seek his word.

This topic is uncomfortable. You rarely hear sermons in mainline denominations where a pastor tackles the subject of false spirits, but hurting people still toy with shady dominions. Consider a person who never got to say goodbye to a loved one and seeks closure from a conversation over a crystal ball.

Be advised any voices heard in a commercial setting such as this aren't authorized by God. "Anyone who does these things is detestable to the Lord" (Deuteronomy 18:12). There is a spiritual realm, and not all of it is benign. Any temptation to grab insights beyond what the Bible reveals puts a person in unprotected territory.

If you have made a mistake and participated in seances or consulted horoscopes and such, it would be a good idea to let God know you are sorry and will not do so again. That way, any ill effects can be cancelled by the covering Jesus creates for cleansing. "If we confess our sins, he is faithful and just and will forgive us our sins and purify us from all unrighteousness" (1 John 1:9).

The book of 1 Samuel relates the story of a man who started in obscurity, then ascended to royalty, only to lose it all. Saul began as an impressive man who stood a head taller than any other Israelite (1 Samuel 9:2). While searching for lost donkeys, he encountered the

---

37 Fash, "How Much Does a Psychic Cost?" https://fash.com/costs/psychic-cost.

respected prophet Samuel, who pulled him aside to reveal Saul would be made king. "The Spirit of the Lord will come powerfully on you, and you will prophesy with them; and you will be changed into a different person" (1 Samuel 10:6).

When the elderly Samuel set up a ceremony to acknowledge the new regent formally, Saul hid by stored supplies (1 Samuel:10:20-23). Did Saul have a case of nerves about public speaking or did he feel in his heart he was unworthy? The Bible doesn't say. What is told is Saul's reign was clouded. God ached because his people preferred an intermediary instead of him.

Samuel predicted Saul would become changed after encountering God. How is your intimacy with God? If you set aside time regularly with just him, you will develop closeness. This relationship is personal and begins inviting Jesus into your life. God yearns to speak with you as an individual.

Though worshipping at church, fellowshipping with prayer groups, and singing with Christian radio are great resources, there is no substitute for sitting in the family room and sharing your thoughts with God himself. He loves your companionship and wants to be with you.

Saul's leadership debut occurred at age 30 when he led 330,000 men against the Ammonites, who threatened to gouge out the right eye of every Israelite man (1 Samuel 11:1-2). God blessed Saul and enabled his army to rout the enemy.

Saul may have been a novice general, but with God's strategy, he had enormous success. You can too. Are you seeking God for wisdom?

Saul gave God the credit: "... for this day the Lord has rescued Israel" (1 Samuel 11:13). Note the humility with which Saul fielded success. He didn't beat his chest and stomp around like a sumo wrestler. With dignity, he honored God.

Soon, however, his faith was challenged. Doubt crept in when Saul faced an invasion by Philistines. Like angry hornets spilling from a nest, the enemy swarmed Israel with far superior numbers. "The

Philistines assembled to fight Israel, with three thousand chariots, six thousand charioteers, and soldiers as numerous as the sand on the seashore" (1 Samuel 13:5).

The Israelites panicked. They failed to call on God for help. Instead of standing in faith and praying, they ran and hid in caves, thickets, and cisterns. Saul may have felt an ulcer developing as he awaited Samuel's instructions in Gilgal. A week went by with no word. When Israelite soldiers started deserting, Saul had a choice to make. Would he trust God to deliver or would he resort to his own devices?

In crisis, what do you do? Do you ask God for guidance and wait for his direction or do you blindly create your own best solution and rashly proceed?

To raise confidence in his troops, Saul implemented his plan without consulting God. He staged a showy sacrifice of burnt offerings and masqueraded as the priest in Samuel's absence. With this ceremony, Saul created a façade of control, all the while ignoring the tremendous power of a heartfelt personal petition to God.

Saul's lack of faith and false pretense violated God's guidance to wait on him. Samuel arrived as the smell of burnt meat wafted across the makeshift altar. "What have you done?" Samuel asked (1 Samuel 13:11).

Saul tried to varnish his behavior. "When I saw the men were scattering, and that you did not come at the set time, and that the Philistines were assembling at Mikmash, I thought, 'Now the Philistines will come down against me at Gilgal, and I have not sought the Lord's favor.' So I felt compelled to offer the burnt offering" (1 Samuel 13:11-12).

His feeble attempt to place blame on Samuel for being late, and justify faking priestly authority to serve God, didn't go over well. Samuel could see right through the half truths. Saul's deceptive language to camouflage his willfulness hid nothing from the prophet.

"You have done a foolish thing," Samuel said (1 Samuel 13:13).

Have you taken matters in your own hands because God seemed to take too long to give the answer you wanted? Rushing into places where you don't have the proper authority to act can be disastrous. Full of bluster, you charge into a situation God hasn't asked you to enter. Maybe like Saul, you are more worried about your reputation than following orders. You encamp on former victories empowered by God and assume you've still got the situation in hand.

King Saul fell from grace because he was dishonest. He felt maintaining an illusion was more important than waiting for God. If you step away from God's commands, don't expect his favor to follow your unapproved agendas. Absolute integrity is what God expects. Even in fearsome circumstances, God wants his beloved to hold their ground because they trust him to deliver. Remaining steadfast during adversity demonstrates depth of faith.

If you make a mistake, admit the error publicly and to God. Repent, which means to turn away from bad behavior. This is the only way to restore trust. God doesn't expect you to be perfect, but he wants you to confess wrongdoing.

God gave Saul another opportunity to demonstrate obedience. He instructed Saul to attack the Amalekites and destroy everything, including their livestock (1 Samuel 15:3). Saul's troops vanquished their enemy, but then they kept the best of the livestock for themselves. Saul didn't stop their plundering. He allowed them to keep the spoils though he knew that wasn't what God ordered.

Amid the loud bleating of confiscated sheep and lowing of cattle, the white-haired Samuel entered the scene and asked Saul what was going on. Samuel knew the answer because God had already told him. He wanted to see if Saul would be honest.

Unfortunately, Saul fabricated another justification. "The soldiers took sheep and cattle from the plunder, the best of what was devoted to God, in order to sacrifice them to the Lord your God at Gilgal" (1 Samuel 15:21).

The fib didn't amuse Samuel. He said, "For rebellion is like the sin of divination, and arrogance like the evil of idolatry. Because you have rejected the word of the Lord, he has rejected you as king" (1 Samuel 15:23). Samuel turned his back on Saul, and the first king of Israel's refusal to be candid and obedient cost him the crown.

Have there been times you ignored what the Holy Spirit told you to do? To look good in front of others, have you twisted facts to align with the impression you wanted to make?

Though God can forgive a lie, he won't bless someone who chooses a pattern of deceit and shows no remorse. "Whoever can be trusted with very little can also be trusted much, and whoever is dishonest with very little will also be dishonest with much" (Luke 16:10). God told Samuel to anoint the young son of Jesse, David, as the new king instead.

Without Samuel's steadying presence, Saul's behavior deteriorated. He brought David into his court, then tried to murder him. Saul continued being two-faced. God left Saul to his depravity but protected the obedient David.

When Philistines again gathered forces to attack Israel, Saul panicked. Since Samuel had died, Saul didn't know what to do. "He inquired of the Lord, but the Lord did not answer him by dreams or Urim or prophets" (1 Samuel 28:6). When he didn't get any word from God, Saul told his attendants to find a medium with whom he could consult the dead (1 Samuel 28:7). Saul again used underhanded means to serve his own purpose.

In a bizarre twist, Saul disguised himself and visited a woman in Endor (1 Samuel 28:8-12). She feared for her life as Saul previously banned mediums and spiritists from Israel with a death penalty if they returned. Saul demanded she call up Samuel's spirit and promised he wouldn't harm her.

Saul didn't get the answers he sought and died the next day in battle. God issues a grave warning about tampering with darks arts: "I will set my face against anyone who turns to mediums and spiritists to prostitute themselves by following them, and I will cut them off from their people" (Leviticus 20:6).

The only true source of knowledge comes from God and his Bible. Scrambling for information from anywhere else will lead to destruction. There are no shortcuts to truth.

Deception was the alligator that ate Saul's soul and led to his demise. Falsehood might appear harmless, but submerged below the surface is the willful disobedience God abhors. Without integrity, Saul slid into dark practices.

Do you feel you are in a stalemate in this season? If so, evaluate for any falsehood in your life. You need to clean house and confess any lies before God. He already knows the truth. He wants to extend mercy, not punishment.

One lesson from Saul's life is to guard against being dishonest. When you sneak around, the only person you fool is yourself. Saul failed to build a personal relationship with God. This spiritual deafness prevented him from receiving the course correction he needed to detour around swamps.

If you hear the distinctive deep, double grunt of a gator in the lake, don't go charging ahead thinking, *I've got this.* Thrashing through thick cattail reeds and wading through slippery mud isn't wise.

Even small lies take on a life of their own. Consider how a hatchling can grow. Female gators can reach 10 feet, and the Florida record weight for a 13 ½-foot-long male is 1,043 pounds.[38] These mottled reptiles can stay underwater for more than two hours.[39] Though appearing sleepy, when they strike, they can reach speeds up

38 Florida Fish and Wildlife Conservation Commission, "Alligator Facts," https://myfwc.com/wildlifehabitats/wildlife/alligator/facts/

39 Florida Alligator Marketing and Education, Bureau of Seafood and Aquaculture Marketing: Tallahassee, FL, "Alligator Facts," https://www.florida-alligator.com/General-Information/Alligator-Facts.

to 35 miles per hour on land and swim up to 20 miles per hour.[40] A falsehood is as powerful as these beasts with 80 teeth.[41]

Similar to alligators, occult practices are hidden dangers. Never approach or feed these creatures, and leave alligator removal to licensed trappers. Your best bet is to stay away—your life may depend on it. Just as state laws forbid interaction with wildlife and keep people away from danger, so do God's rules against toying with witchcraft or astrology keep you safe.

God promises if you call out to him, he will answer you and tell you great and unsearchable things you do not know (Jeremiah 33:3).

FOR REFLECTION

"The acts of the flesh are obvious: sexual immorality, impurity and debauchery; idolatry and witchcraft; hatred, discord, jealousy, fits of rage, selfish ambition, dissensions, factions and envy; drunkenness, orgies, and the like. I warn you, as I did before, that those who live like this will not inherit the kingdom of God" (Galatians 5:19-21).

The lesson from Saul's life is to guard against dishonesty that takes you down a dank spiral of disobedience. Refrain from speaking half truths. "Do not lie. Do not deceive one another" (Leviticus 19:11). Seek integrity in all you do.

Saul failed to build a personal relationship with God and depended on others for hearing guidance. This spiritual deafness prevented

---

40 Experience Kissimme, "7 Surprising Facts about Alligators You Didn't Know,"March 20, 2020, https://www.experiencekissimmee.com/blog/7-alligator-facts-you-probably-didnt-know.

41 Florida Alligator Marketing and Education, Bureau of Seafood and Aquaculture Marketing: Tallahassee, FL, "Alligator Facts," https://www.florida-alligator.com/General-Information/Alligator-Facts.

Saul from receiving the course correction he needed to detour around swamps.

Do you rely on others to tell you what God wants? Though conferring with wise, godly counselors can be beneficial, God wants *you* to communicate directly with him. Take time today to pray and journal what comes to mind. Reviewing this ledger can help you see patterns over time you may otherwise miss.

A PRAYER FOR TODAY

Dear Lord, Please forgive me for times I have sought answers in sources other than you. I am sorry for seeking power to elevate myself. You are the only source of truth. Though I may yearn to know more about the future, I trust you to reveal the knowledge when the time is right. I will not seek false sources. Please help me develop a stronger personal relationship with you. Amen

Chapter Fifteen

GENTLE GUIDANCE

*H*ouse sitting requires the ultimate in trust. Whom do you allow in your home when you aren't there to care for your most precious things? You must choose carefully who is responsible enough to spritz the prized orchid, clean the hamster cage, and stack mail on the kitchen counter.

Though you leave a detailed list, there is always something you might forget. In those instances, you count on the observant eye of someone who cares and notices what needs to be done. Thank goodness, your friend spies the orange goldfish circling the bowl looking hungry. Your house sitter drops in five brown pellets, which swiftly are vacuumed up.

When Jesus departed the earthly realm to return to heaven, he designated the Holy Spirit to take care of things until his return. If you have accepted Jesus into your life, you have invited him to live with you internally—and eternally. "Do you not know that your bodies are temples of the Holy Spirit, who is in you, whom you have received from God?" (1 Corinthians 6:19). Your physical being is a cathedral of the most intricate dressed bone, and your eyes are colorful windows of stained glass. Your voice praising God is the organ playing hymns. As his special domain, you benefit from insights, cautions, and coaching the Holy Spirit offers from the holy altar of your heart.

While some might feel awkward discussing an invisible being, there is no need. You talk on a cell phone to people you can't see and email acquaintances around the globe. Those virtual communications are no less important than face-to-face ones. Just because the Holy Spirit's presence is intangible like the wind doesn't make his input invalid. A gentle breeze can caress your cheek, and a gale can topple sturdy trees. You can't hold the wind, but you certainly can see its effects.

Jesus specifically asked God to provide a counselor to help you determine truth and be with you forever (John 14:16). Sometimes, the Holy Spirit's ethereal majesty makes feeling close to him difficult. Perhaps thinking of the Holy Spirit as a dear neighbor is a creative way to draw closer to him.

Pretend you give him an extra set of keys for your house because your trust in him is solid. He looks out for you, even when you are unaware. Picture a guy in his 50s who wears a white T-shirt and clean but worn jeans. His figure is trim, but his biceps bulge like inflated blood-pressure cuffs. He maintains a low profile and never draws attention to himself. You've nicknamed the Holy Spirit "Henry," as the two of you set aside formalities long ago.

Maybe a distinctive tattoo on his right forearm shows a scarlet heart with a white lamb in the center. On the lamb's head is a shiny golden crown. Henry's salt-and-pepper crew cut hints at military background, though he seldom talks about his war experiences. You've wanted to ask him if he led a battalion when Gabriel needed reinforcements during the Persian campaign to help Daniel (Daniel 10:13). However, you hesitate to bring up bad memories.

Henry enjoys protecting you and sharing wisdom he's gained along the way because he's seen a lot of action. He trained 70 of Israel's leaders to set up the new nation (Numbers 11:16-17). Even if you need help with homework, Henry's knowledge about history and science is impressive. After all, he saw the formation of the world (Genesis 1:1-2). As your close friend and confidante, Henry will teach you all things and remind you of everything Jesus has said (John 14:26). Henry models several desirable attributes:

Respectful: Henry doesn't show up at your place and start tearing out the carpet and redesigning the kitchen. You won't come home and see polka-dotted spray paint on the walls or a rock garden in what used to be a lush lawn. While Henry may suggest renovations to add appeal, he awaits your authorization. He allows you space to decide what you are willing to try. He shares God's commands and points out circumstances where these principles apply to everyday circumstances.

Henry honors your privacy. He is not a nosy neighbor who sneaks around trying to get the scoop on your shortcomings to post on social media. He keeps your confidences and makes no judgment when you disclose the tub has rings and the toilet hasn't been scrubbed in months. He will frown at your little white lie spoken at work and fold his arms. Then he'll grab cleaning supplies and stand with you to fix issues.

Neither will Henry rifle through your office paperwork and *tsk tsk* about bills due. The Holy Spirit may suggest you take 10 percent off the top of your paycheck and share with your church, charity, or a family in need, but he won't demand that. The Counselor quietly refrains from your personal matters until you allow him to double-check balances and establish payment plans for debts. He can offer reasonable solutions to financial dilemmas using God's guidance, but he won't be bossy. When you need to forgive someone or repay a debt, Henry may hold the calculator, but he lets you sign the check.

Capable: Life is full of surprises, like when an AC unit conks out in 90-degree temperatures or when the Labrador gobbles up a bag of chocolate cookies stolen from the counter. A house sitter is someone you can rely on to deal with emergencies. Henry's contact list is infinite. He can whip out his phone in the blink of an eye and have help on the way. If you need a plumber, he will guide you to a reliable person. Lonely and looking for a hobby to meet other people? Henry can facilitate that. Even if you have to remember how to do

Cardiopulmonary Resuscitation when a stranger at the grocery store collapses, Henry participates in the buddy system and alternates compressing the person's chest.

Henry is cool as ice on a summer day when you want to panic. He will bring to mind the steps to walk you through what you need to do. Henry prompts others to check on you and see what you need. Ever "had a feeling" to slow down at a busy intersection, only to miss being T-boned by a car running the red light? The *only* time Henry yells is if danger is imminent. If you sense "Watch out." "Stay away from that building." Or "Avoid that person." Respond immediately. Henry's job is to protect. He's a night owl, early bird, and everything in between, so you never need to worry about interrupting his schedule.

Punctual: Your buddy Henry arrives right on time. He doesn't show up early and put you in a tailspin. The Holy Spirit makes his entrance when you are ready to receive him, and he's been bailing people out for more than millennia. There's no situation he hasn't already seen. Job loss. Check. Flood. Check. Dying loved one. Check. Henry has perfected the ability to say exactly the right thing at the right moment. You may not want to hear what he has to say, but you know he has your best interests in mind. If you are playing around with a bad choice, he won't hesitate to tap you on the shoulder and say, "Dude. Have you really thought this through?" Even if you ignore him and make a dumb choice, he will stick with you to resolve the problem, if you let him. He isn't into perfection, but he is into purification.

Virtuous: Another characteristic of Henry is his sterling reputation as honorable. You don't have to worry that while you are at work, Henry will throw the party of the century and invite all the crazies to trash your house. He won't toss beer bottles behind your hedge or leave smelly trash in the kitchen for a week. Henry associates with people of integrity. And if you take the time to ask him, Henry can help you steer clear of trouble. He has great discernment for peoples' motives. He may raise an eyebrow at someone new you bring home. Pay attention because he sees beyond façades to the heart.

Gentle: Though Henry is powerful, he doesn't run roughshod over you. The Counselor doesn't beat you over the head, saying "Hey, dummy, don't you get it?" Henry acts like a gentleman. He puts into practice: "The Lord's servant must not be quarrelsome but must be kind to everyone, able to teach, not resentful" (2 Timothy 2:24). The Holy Spirit gently instructs you to improve your outlook and actions. Henry models wisdom that is pure, peace-loving, considerate, merciful, and sincere (James 3:17). He speaks truth, and he does it in such a way you taste sweets to savor instead of hot sauce to spit out. The Counselor is an essential part of the regal trinity, but he serves as boots on the ground to advise you in daily circumstances.

God promises he will send the Holy Spirit to guide you into all truth (John 16:1).

FOR REFLECTION

"Which of you fathers, if your son asks for a fish, will give him a snake instead? Or if he asks for an egg, will give him a scorpion. If you then, though you are evil, know how to give good gifts to your children, how much more will your Father in heaven give the Holy Spirit to those who ask him!" (Luke 11:11-13).

Ever take time to wrap a present in colorful paper and tie the bow just so. You can't wait to see the recipient's excitement. The only problem is your carefully chosen gift is ignored. That may be how God feels when he sends the Holy Spirit to comfort and advise you, but you refuse to participate in any dialogue.

The Holy Spirit's presence is one to comfort and protect you. What obstacles prevent you from trusting him more fully?

A PRAYER FOR TODAY

Dear Lord, Thank you for sending the Counselor to lead me in your paths. Please teach me how to recognize the gentle prompts of your Spirit. Show me how to discern (test) impressions I receive that go beyond what may seem ordinary. I want only to bring you honor through loving actions. Amen

Chapter Sixteen

RULES FOR THE ROAD

*T*hese days, people focus on what they're entitled to much more than for what they should be responsible. Loud, snarky voices are quick to demand what they want, but that isn't God's way. He establishes order so the world can run smoothly. Think of what would happen on a highway if drivers chose whatever lane they wanted and went any speed, without following rules. Northbound traffic would collide with southern travelers. Vehicles would pass on the shoulders, and speed-demons would weave in and out of lanes without regard for others. (Sounds too much like the interstate you travel every day, huh?)

There are reasons for rules. Without them, screeching tires would be heard and burnt rubber would blacken pavement. There would be pile-ups, and wrecks would litter the landscape. Sirens would scream, and rescuers would be overwhelmed trying to get to those needing attention. Just as drivers must learn to obey directions for the well-being of all, so should God's people follow a code of conduct.

In Exodus 20 and Deuteronomy 5, God spells out clearly rules of the road for his followers. He establishes ten commandments to secure communities. These can be likened to the road signs of today. Each symbol represents guidance to keep you safe.

1. God says he is your Lord and you shall have no other gods before him (Exodus 20:2-3 and Deuteronomy 5:6-7).
The foundation for all commandments is putting aside self to please

117

God. You willingly surrender whatever direction you prefer and travel his way. For example, you take a few extra moments in the morning to listen to a co-worker who is struggling. Answering emails can wait a bit. Another opportunity to go God's way may be praying at 3 a.m. if you get a gentle nudge to intercede for someone.

Going in God's traffic pattern often involves a thousand "inconveniences." However, without these small acts of obedience, you'll never develop the discipline to be faithful in larger tasks. "Not my will, but yours be done," Jesus said as he relinquished privilege and accepted suffering in the Mount of Olives (Luke 22:42).

You give up trying to control your destiny, trusting God has good in store for you. Rather than requesting God bless whatever choices you make, you kneel quietly in prayer and ask him to show you the road he chooses for you. Then you proceed where he instructs.

Devotion solely to God requires bypassing enticements of pride and social acclaim on side streets. Jesus counseled the disciples, "Whoever wants to be my disciple must deny themselves and take up their cross daily and follow me" (Luke 9:23). Loving God is a series of decisions each day to obey—not out of fear, but love.

Having no other gods means you weigh every alternative by what honors the Lord as your foremost concern. "Seek first his kingdom and his righteousness" (Matthew 6:33). Every choice is a window framing how important God is to you. Are you looking ahead? You set aside what you want and follow his one-way guidance. This is a sweet sacrifice. "Love the Lord your God with all your heart and with all your soul and with all your strength" (Deuteronomy 6:5).

2. God says you shall not make idols or bow down and worship anything except him (Exodus 20:4 and Deuteronomy 5:8).

You are going the wrong way on an exit ramp if you pursue anything that is a higher priority than God. Career, financial success, family, and social standing are worthy causes, but none of them will turn out if you aren't right with God first.

Maybe you say to yourself, *If I work weekends and make this promotion, then I will have enough money to slow down and go back to church soon.* Nope. That notion is mistaken. The nameplate on a swanky office suite is an idol if it takes your eyes off the Lord. God is jealous, and he doesn't want the leftovers of your life (Deuteronomy 5:9). He wants prime time.

Another distraction could be your adorable children as you run them all over kingdom come for dance classes, athletic events, and slumber parties. You cater to their social calendar to the point you never have a moment to study the Bible or pray. You only have so much energy to go around. If you chase a daily agenda bereft of God, soon all you have are grumpy, exhausted kids. Scratching your head, you try to figure out went wrong when all you wanted to do was give them the best. God is the best, and the most awesome childhood experience you can offer young ones is the realization he is present in every moment.

Even worthy community activities can become an "idol" if you do the volunteering without God. Though the exterior appearance may be of commitment to charity, exercise caution your involvement doesn't hide a secret desire for personal recognition about your noble efforts. Every action that takes away from God's glory is in the wrong direction.

3. God says you shall not misuse his name (Exodus 20:7 and Deuteronomy 5:11).

You enter a no-passing zone when you take God's name in vain. There is no need for cursing or profanity. These crude habits resemble fingernail screeches on an old chalkboard, and they offend God. Stay in your lane and be respectful.

People also don't need to exaggerate promises or swear on the Bible to prove their integrity. "Do not swear—not by heaven or by earth or by anything else," James advised disciples in the New Testament. "All you need to say is a simple 'Yes' or 'No'" (James 5:12). If anyone waxes poetic and swears on the Bible to do so and so, you should run. Honest people make a commitment and don't belabor the point.

You also want to preserve admiration for a holy God. People in countries with sovereign leaders such as England or Jordan understand centuries of tradition to be honored with titles. Can you imagine the shock in the court if someone sidled up to the monarch, clapped him on the shoulder saying, "Hey, bubba. How ya doin'?" Attendants would have cardiac arrest. No one would address the king or queen by first name in a too-familiar manner. Their office commands deference for those who want to approach the throne, and the same is true for God. Though he encourages you to converse with him, keep in mind he is royal.

Jewish tradition holds the name of God is so precious no one is supposed to speak it out loud. According to *The Compass* in a 2009 article, the Vatican directed U.S. bishops refrain from saying the name "Yahweh" in services out of respect.[42] "Yahweh is a spoken word that comes from the four consonants of the ancient Hebrew language that represent the divine name of God."[43] *The Compass* editor further explained Jews believed this name to be so holy the average person only heard it spoken aloud once a year.

Only the high priest could utter this precious name on the Day of Atonement in the presence of the Holy of the Holies while sprinkling blood on the mercy seat to atone for sins.[44] As the sacrifice for all sins to make people clean, Jesus holds a sacred position. Please recognize his authority by treating his name with honor.

4. God says to remember the Sabbath day and keep it holy (Exodus 20:8 and Deuteronomy 5:12).

This sign lists the maximum recommended safe speed for an exit ramp, but life's frantic pace often pushes out time for rest and reflection. You get so busy doing, doing, doing, you are breathless. Each

---

42 Catholic Diocese of Green Bay, Wisconsin, *The Compass*, "The Name That Must Not Be Said Out Loud," January 20, 2009, https://www.thecompassnews.org/2009/01/the-name-that-must-not-be-said-out-loud/ (*accessed* April 3, 2021).

43 Ibid.

44 Ibid.

night when you collapse at home, you wonder what you've really achieved. Time to rest. You need a mental health break. Step aside from constant movement and sigh with relief as you put up your feet on the couch. This is an opportunity to process everything that's been going on. Look for ways to reconnect with God. Unplug from all the other demands to reset your mind on him.

"Six days you shall labor and do all your work, but the seventh day is a Sabbath to the Lord your God. On it you shall not do any work" (Deuteronomy 5:13-14). God knows you get weary. He realizes the body and mind need an opportunity to rest. This command isn't designed to be punitive, but restorative. For many whose jobs require weekend work, God wants at least one 24-hour period to be free of obligations. There has to be some down time to refill your reservoir of peace before you go back to worldly challenges. If you are running on empty, then you have little to give.

5. God says you are to honor your father and mother (Exodus 20:12 and Deuteronomy 5:16).

You must slow down and give vehicles crossing your path the right-of-way. Showing respect is a way to put others before yourself. This selflessness reflects a desire to look out for people God puts in your sphere of influence. Biological and adoptive parents have the incredible task of nurturing a new life and ensuring a child has a safe upbringing. Parents are soldiers who defend innocents against peril.

Some adults do a fabulous job in this role. They are nurturing, steadfast, and effective guiding children to the precepts that establish a good life. Unfortunately, some parents have their own issues and fall short. But either way, you are to show respect to the adults who are part of your life. "Honor your father and your mother, as the Lord your God has commanded you, so that you may live long and that it may go well with you in the land the Lord your God is giving you" (Deuteronomy 5:16). The command comes with blessings: full life and a place of belonging.

Even if your parents are gone and you have no biological children, you serve as a spiritual parent for new believers who observe your life. Modeling politeness sets a good tone for interactions. "Listen, my son, to your father's instruction and do not forsake your mother's teaching," counsels Proverbs 1:8-9. "They are a garland to grace your head and a chain to adorn your neck." Godly parents and adults give precious presents when they share gems of wisdom with younger generations. This heritage is one to be treasured.

6. God says you shall not murder (Exodus 20:13 and Deuteronomy 5:17).

You must bring your vehicle to a complete halt at the crosswalk or stop line. In a similar manner, you need to control your thoughts and statements to avoid injuring another. Failing to stop anger causes destruction like a fast-moving car hitting a pedestrian. Jesus said, "But I tell you that anyone who is angry with a brother or sister will be subject to judgment" (Matthew 5:22).

In rage's heat, saying hateful words or maintaining a stony silence create wounds as life-threatening as a knife stab to the heart. "The tongue has the power of life and death" (Proverbs 18:21). What you say impacts lives. Though you may never consider physically attacking another human, you may damage them with verbal weapons.

An online law site defines murder as a crime planned with malice.[45] The perpetrator has time to reflect, yet still kills. This dangerous pattern can be seen in relationships when one person is bent on harming another. Consider a corporate rivalry where one member unjustly assassinates the character of a competitor. God will arrest this unauthorized climb for "success."

He also frowns on unkind remarks about neighbors or fellow church members. Jealousy can be a flashing yellow light. "Do not be like Cain, who belonged to the evil one and murdered his brother.

---

45 Sara J. Berman, NOLO, "What is Murder?" https://www.nolo.com/legal-encyclopedia/homicide-murder-manslaughter-32637.html, (accessed April 2, 2021).

And why did he murder him? Because his own actions were evil and his brother's were righteous" (1 John 3:12). Keeping vigil on your own actions and heart is a full-time job. Don't waste time comparing yourself with others.

Proverbs extends the danger zones to include: haughty eyes (feeling superior to others); a lying tongue; hands that shed innocent blood; and a heart that devises wicked schemes (Proverbs 6:16-17). When envy rears its head, stop the vehicle immediately to prevent needless loss. Look both ways and ensure God will be pleased.

7. God says you shall not commit adultery (Exodus 20:14 and Deuteronomy 5:18).

As a wedding ring marks a special arrangement, so do diamond-shaped signs indicate a lane reserved for certain purposes. In God's design, marriage protects you from getting snarled up in lanes of unhealthy desires that fuel lust and undermine integrity. "Can a man scoop fire into his lap without his clothes being burned?" challenges Proverbs 6:27 about lusting after a woman's beauty. "Can a man walk on hot coals without his feet being scorched? So is he who sleeps with another man's wife; no one who touches her will go unpunished" (Proverbs 6:28-29).

For a married couple, sexuality is a glorious and wondrous sharing. This physical connection unites a man and woman, seals a covenant, and bonds souls. This sacred act is diminished by media messages bombarding you about passionate hook-ups without a care in the world or lasting connection. The falsehood isn't realized until too late with unpleasant consequences. "But the man who commits adultery has no sense; whoever does so destroys himself" (Proverbs 6:32).

Flirtation with a co-worker may stroke ego, but why toy with others' emotions to fuel the altar of self worship? Jesus said, "Anyone who looks at a woman lustfully has already committed adultery with her in his heart" (Matthew 5:28). Seems fair women will be held to the same standard. Roving eyes gaze upon trouble.

Disclosing unflattering personal information about your spouse in a public setting violates his or her privacy. Is getting a quick laugh at your partner's expense something to be proud of? "Marriage should be honored by all, and the marriage bed kept pure, for God will judge the adulterer and all the sexually immoral" (Hebrews 13:4).

Keeping home matters cordoned off keeps both spouses feeling safe and valued. "Let him kiss me with the kisses of his mouth—for your love is more delightful than wine" (Song of Songs 1:2).

In a committed marriage, love is pleasing and satisfying. "Show me your face, let me hear your voice; for your voice is sweet, and your face is lovely" (Song of Songs 2:14). To protect yourself from tempting distractions, gaze only in the eye of your beloved. There you will observe lifelong adoration rather than a fleeting pass.

8. God says you shall not steal (Exodus 20:15 and Deuteronomy 5:19).

The do not enter sign is on one-way streets. Respect others' property. This includes ideas and territory. Robbing a jewelry store at gunpoint is an obvious crime, but how many times do employees make personal copies on the company machine or take long lunches? These *smaller* offenses show an attitude of *me-first* and doesn't set well with God. He expects his children to show integrity in everything.

What about intellectual property? Do you take credit for an idea someone else had instead of praising them for the awesome contribution?

Trampling on another person's dreams and aspirations is just as bad. God may tap someone to an unusual destiny to bring him glory. He is excited to have a "nobody" do the impossible. An unknown musician strumming a guitar in the middle of the night brings forth a praise song that hits the top of the chart. An ice skater makes a comeback in the Olympics. The world needs champions to show how to overcome.

These pioneers need encouragers who believe in them early on and sustain them during the climb. When God established the Israelites as a new nation, he said, "I myself have selected your fellow Levites from among the Israelites as a gift to you, dedicated to the Lord to do the work at the tent of Meeting" (Numbers 18:6). True service is about what you give, not what you take. Do not enter a lane for yourself, but look instead where you can facilitate the transit of someone moving toward God.

9. God says you shall not give false testimony against your neighbor (Exodus 20:16 and Deuteronomy 5:20).

You must not turn either to the right or to the left at this intersection. Stay true to accuracy in recounting events. God detests "A false witness who pours out lies" (Proverbs 6:19). There is no need to speak against others to make yourself look better. Be known as the person at the office or club who is a straight shooter and tells it like it is. People value directness and honesty. These qualities sound simple, but they require discipline and courage to implement.

Have you had a gossip pigeonhole you and blab on and on about a juicy tidbit? This rumormonger takes joy in spreading sorrow. If you are a willing audience, take heed, because anything you might share will be passed along for entertainment later to someone else.

"Acquitting the guilty and condemning the innocent—the Lord detests them both" (Proverbs 17:15). In a courtroom, witnesses must swear to tell the whole truth and nothing but the truth. This foundation ensures fairness, which is important in determining if a charge is legitimate. Jumping to conclusions or seeing only partial presentation of facts leaves you with inadequate information for decisions. Allow dialogue with family members and colleagues to ensure there is full understanding. There always is more than one side to consider.

10. God says you shall not covet anything belonging to your neighbor (Exodus 20:17 and Deuteronomy 5:21).

Your speed must not exceed the posted limit. You look longingly at your co-worker's car and contrast her shiny new model with yours. Neighbors just got a new Samsung Wall MicroLED TV that spans 292 inches. You consider how that might look in your family room during football season. A passerby has on an impressive outfit, and you wish you had the extra cash to pull off the ensemble. None of these wishes is bad. However, danger lies in you wanting more, more, more. Acquiring possessions can become a merry-go-round leaving you dizzy and sick.

Gratitude is the antidote to desiring what others have. If you are busy thanking God for what he's given you, then you don't have time to worry about what else is out there that may tickle your fancy. McMansions are gorgeous, but maintenance expenses can create ulcers if the mortgage already strains your budget to the breaking point. The Joneses will not help you pay down the principal. Trying to keep up with them isn't worth bankruptcy.

Diamonds sparkle almost as much as the gleam in the salesperson's eyes, particularly if you finance a payment plan with high interest. However, saving up cash for purchases has no glamor at all. In fact, delayed gratification makes you really add up how much a whim can cost. Calculate how many hours you have to work to buy something. Are you going to enjoy the acquisition for longer than the payoff takes?

God wants to bless you with wonderful things, but he will ensure items don't become heavy burdens. Jesus assures you whatever you need will be provided. "Ask and it will be given to you; seek and you will find; knock and the door will be opened to you" (Matthew 7:7 and Luke 11:9). Trust him to deliver good gifts. There is no need to grasp for second-rate substitutes.

ର ର ର ର ର

The Ten Commandments are promises more than restrictions. They are invitations to God's highway where one can travel without fear. As every driver knows, there will be times when violations occur. The speedometer races, the double-line gets crossed, and the stop sign ignored. Rather than beat yourself up for these infractions, acknowledge your mistake and try to do better. As it is written: "There is no one righteous, not even one" (Romans 3:10).

God is not a law enforcement officer bent on jailing you. Instead, he is a patrolman who has responded to many wrecks with shattered lives. He wants to educate you about safety protocol so you will mature and operate with prudence. All fall short of the glory of God, but he graciously redeems us through Jesus (Romans 3:24-26). Next time you get behind the wheel, offer a prayer, asking God to help you see the road signs ahead and follow their instructions.

God promises if you will follow his decrees and are careful to obey his commands, he will grant peace in the land and no one will make you afraid (Leviticus 26:3-6).

FOR REFLECTION

"Children, obey your parents in the Lord, for this is right. Honor your father and mother—which is the first commandment with a promise—so that it may go well with you and that you may enjoy long life on the earth. Fathers, do not exasperate your children; instead, bring them up in the training and instruction of the Lord" (Ephesians 6:1-4).

God's rules are not capricious dictates to feed his ego. Instead, they are commonsense guidelines for establishing orderly and peaceful communities. When you review every choice in light of pleasing him, you follow a path of integrity. He gives you freedom of choice. When you obey, he blesses your life with abundance.

Of the ten commandments, which is the easiest for you to follow? Why? Which is the most difficult? Reflect how you can shore up areas of weakness. Perhaps seeking an accountability partner who is confidential and trustworthy can help you change destructive patterns.

A PRAYER FOR TODAY

Dear Lord, Ten rules don't seem like much, but I break them regularly. Please help me do better. When I am tempted to give in to road rage and think the world revolves around my wants, please flash that caution light so I will slow down and not sin. Thank you Jesus for making a way for me even when I miss direction. Amen

Chapter Seventeen

LIVING WATER

$\mathcal{S}$tanding in the shower, hot water pulses down your back with wonderful pressure. Steam rises, and your toes get a little pruney as you luxuriate in the cleansing flow. The scent of body wash perfumes the air as you scrub. Little bubbles vanish down the drain, taking with them the day's sweat and dirt.

Contrast that pleasant experience with being outside and the temperature exceeds 90 degrees Fahrenheit. No shade exists. You tilt up your canteen to parched and cracked lips, ready for a sip of refreshing water, only to realize the container is dry as a desert fossil. Sunburn cooks your face.

A person only can survive about three days without adequate fluids.[46] Symptoms of dehydration vary by age and overall health, but common ones include dry mouth and little or darkening urine. Dehydration is easy to remedy early on but can be serious if left unchecked.[47] Water is necessary to regulate body temperature, aid in digestion, balance body pH, lubricate joints, deliver oxygen, and eliminate waste.[48]

---

46 Jon Johnson, Medical News Today, "How Long Can You Live Without Water," May 14, 2019, https://www.medicalnewstoday.com/articles/325174#:~:text=As%20a%20general%20rule%20 of,uses%20water%2C%20can%20affect%20this (*accessed* April 5, 2021).

47 Peter Crosta, Medical News Today, "What You Should Know about Dehydration," December 20, 2017, https://www.medicalnewstoday.com/articles/325174#how-long-can-you-live-without-water (*accessed* April 5, 2021).

48 Jon Johnson, Medical News Today, "How Long Can You Live Without Water," May 14, 2019, https://www.medicalnewstoday.com/articles/325174#:~:text=As%20a%20general%20rule%20 of,uses%20water%2C%20can%20affect%20this (*accessed* April 5, 2021).

Having access to plentiful clean water is necessary as a Samaritan woman understood in an ancient town called Sychar. She planned to tote her clay jar to the communal well, drop the rope, and pull up as many gallons as she could carry. She hoped to get enough to cook dinner, clean the dishes, and maybe shampoo her hair.

So intent was she plodding on her hot midday task she didn't see the weary stranger sitting on cistern's edge until she was almost on top of him. He looked scruffy in a travel-stained robe. He sort of wilted in the heat waves, and she felt sorry for him. Why in the world hadn't he brought his own bucket?

Sometimes the supernatural shows up in ordinary settings, and you might miss the miracle. The woman at the well in Sychar almost did. The tired man was none other than Jesus. He asked her, "Will you give me a drink?" (John 4:7). She hesitated as she recognized him as a Jew. Besides, only the two of them stood outside. No passerby should see her with yet another man hanging around. She edged away a bit and pondered her choices.

Hospitality demanded she look after travelers, but common sense told her no right-minded male would ask for her help. She also might have resented the fact a Jewish man treated her like a servant. Maybe she was puzzled. "How can you ask me for a drink?" (John 4:9).

Jesus turned the tables on her by switching from being a petitioner to a benefactor. "If you knew the gift of God and who it is that asks you for a drink, you would have asked him and he would have given you living water" (John 4:10).

The woman may have wondered if this traveler had been out in the sun too long with the riddle he spoke. She looked closer and saw his eyes were clear. Curious, she asked, "Where can you get this living water?" (John 4:11). She was no fool and didn't want to carry endless heavy jars back and forth to the house if she didn't have to. Maybe this guy knew a secret spring he could lead her to.

"Whoever drinks the water I give them will never thirst." (John 4:14).

Now he had her attention. She visualized a waterfall with snow-melted sweetness rushing by. In her imagination, a full stream coursed along banks full of lush vegetation. Weary of barely making ends meet and wanting more, she took a chance. "Sir, give me this water so that I won't get thirsty and have to keep coming here to draw water" (John 4:15).

Jesus used a series of questions to open her mind to possibilities. He didn't start reciting a long-winded sermon and point his finger at her. He interrupted the monotonous daily routine, inviting her to think what was deeply important.

Jesus also may use your dissatisfaction to steer you toward a spring of new knowledge that refreshes and sustains in the dry times. What does your heart seek?

God leaves a channel in each person for life-sustaining water that comes from him alone. Nothing but connection with him will slake your thirst. "My people have committed two sins: They have forsaken me, the spring of living water, and have dug their own cisterns, broken cisterns that cannot hold water" (Jeremiah 2:13).

When you get stuck in a routine and miss God's appointments, you slip into an existence of going through the motions without a satisfying purpose. Too often, we allow tasks to consume most of our time, draining us and leaving us tired.

Jesus wants you to rest and let him refresh you. In Middle Eastern culture, wells served as the focal point for the community. Without one, the people couldn't settle for long. One reference explained naming a well established ownership.[49]

Is there a physical location where you feel the closeness of God? How often do you visit that spot to draw in new inspiration and strength?

---

49 "Well in Fausset's Bible Dictionary," Bible History, https://www.bible-history.com/links.php?cat=39&sub=453&cat_name=Manners+%26+Customs&subcat_name=Wells, (*accessed* April 8, 2021.

Wells also were places of confrontation. Marauders would conquer the territory or stop up the well to drive out settlers. How carefully do you guard your place of renewing? This asset is one that may be easy to take for granted, but without it, you wander in hostile terrain without supply. How do you limit access to your place for spiritual replenishment?

A pastoral message from the United Church of Canada explored the significance of the Water Gate in Jerusalem. After years of exile, the Jews returned to rebuild the destroyed city. "The people then gather at a place called the Water Gate. It stood facing the destroyed temple. Imagine the scene for a moment ... This is the first time in over fifty years that the people of Israel have come together to hear the Torah, the Word of God read in public."[50]

For them, reading the Bible was a major source of renewal. Hearing God's promises spoken aloud reminded them how God kept his covenant. They recommitted themselves to follow his commands and be obedient. You also are invited to find quiet times in the Word where God can minister to you. A quiet soaking in his presence washes away discouragement and fatigue.

As these exiles girded themselves for the reconstruction ahead, they listened as one to God's written word. "Ezra the priest brought the Law before the assembly, which comprised men and women and all who could understand. He read it aloud from daybreak till noon as he faced the square before the Water Gate. And all the people listened attentively to the Book of the Law" (Nehemiah 8:2-3).

Can you imagine asking a modern congregation to stand half a day listening to holy readings? What thirst drove the Jews to drink up every word shared with them?

Wayne Stiles posts online some archaeologists believe the Water Gate stood near the Gihon Spring, which would have been

---

50 "Water Gate and the Word," York-Covehead Pastoral Charge, The United Church of Canada, https://yorkcovehead.wordpress.com/sermons/2019-2/january/water-gate-and-the-word/ (*accessed* April 8, 2021.

Jerusalem's only source of fresh water.[51] He wrote the Jews had the powerful metaphor of provision right in front of them as they heard God's teachings. They saw clear reflections how God's love flowed to meet their needs.

He wants to do the same for you. Are you thirsty? With many choices, you might reach for a soda of entertainment, but that sugary substitute won't fortify you like the pure water of God's word. The coffee of news headlines may startle you awake, but soon the caffeine wears off and you are thirstier than even before for encouragement.

God promises you a dry period won't last forever and his reign will refresh the earth. "Never again will they hunger; never again will they thirst. The sun will not beat down on them, nor any scorching heat. For the lamb at the center of the throne will be their shepherd; he will lead them to springs of living water. And God will wipe away every tear from their eyes" (Revelation 7:16-17).

During drought, keep watch for God's provision and stay in prayer. In 1 Kings 18, the Old Testament prophet Elijah witnessed a three-year drought, but when he prayed, God answered. By persevering in petition, Elijah called forth "a cloud as small as a man's hand is rising from the sea" (1 Kings 18:44). Next thing you know, the sky grew black and a heavy rain fell. Listen for the pitter patter of the refreshing drops of hope his words will bring. You'll splash barefoot in the summer showers of his grace.

> ***God promises if you are thirsty and come to Jesus,***
> ***he will provide rivers of living water***
> ***(John 7:37-38).***

51 Wayne Stiles, "Jerusalem's Water Gate–Where the Source of Truth Gushed," https://waynestiles.com/jerusalems-water-gate-where-the-source-of-truth-gushed-forth/ (*accessed* April 8, 2021).

FOR REFLECTION

"I am the Alpha and the Omega, the Beginning and the End. To the thirsty I will give water without cost from the spring of the water of life" (Revelation 21:6).

"Blessed are those whose strength is in you, whose hearts are set on pilgrimage. As they pass through the Valley of Baka, they make it a place of springs; the autumn rains also cover it with pools. They go from strength to strength, till each appears before God in Zion" (Psalm 84:5-7).

Desert places are where you feel dry and empty, like in the Valley of Baka. You have walked a long distance, yet still don't see the oasis ahead. When you thirst for something more, seek refreshment from God's word.

Life is a pilgrimage, and there will be seasons where rain is scarce. Conserve your energy and sit in the shade of a palm. Take out your Bible and find renewal in God's presence.

Which promise can best sustain you now? How can your life experiences be a testimony to refresh someone else on his or her journey?

A PRAYER FOR TODAY

Dear Lord, I've been eating life's bags of salty peanuts with stale crackers, and I am thirsty. Please show me an oasis spot where I can rest in your shade. I need you. Amen

Chapter Eighteen

ROCKING ON THE PORCH

The old rocking chair creaks a bit as you settle into it. The day's chores are done, and you relax outside to welcome dusk. Birds serenade you with crickets chirping harmony. The cool of the evening embraces you and your shoulders sag in relief. The kitchen is cleaned and the laundry done. No more work this day.

Colors soften as the sun sets. Quiet soothes you. The striving and straining are set aside for rest. Contented, you sit with God beside you like a spouse of many years. No need for words. There's a shared peacefulness you've given your best today, and tomorrow's challenges haven't yet arrived. Just being is enough for this moment.

Your feet push up and down to rock. You hum a little ditty to no particular tune while your mind scrolls through the day. Many of the chores on this morning's to-do list have been checked off. Others remain. That's OK. You'll pick up tomorrow where you left off.

In this space with no duties, you reflect on God's presence with you. You thank him for the successes of this 24-hour period and ask him to guide you tomorrow to do right. As that wicker chair cradles, you feel secure. You may not have all the answers, but you know who does. As God walked with you today, so will he be beside you tomorrow.

The apostle Paul wrote: "I know what it is to be in need, and I know what it is to have plenty. I have learned the secret of being content in any and every situation, whether well fed or hungry, whether living in plenty or in want" (Philippians 4:12). He wrote this to fellow believers in Philippi who had been faithful sending aid. Interestingly, Paul composed this while incarcerated by Romans around 62 A.D.

He had no personal possessions, retirement plan—nor any guarantee he would be released. His status was uncertain. Though he hoped to be reunited soon with friends, he also faced a stark alternative. Historians of the *Encyclopedia Britannica* wrote: "Apprehensive that his execution was close at hand, yet hoping somehow to visit the Philippians again, Paul explains that he was imprisoned for preaching the gospel of Christ."[52]

Easton's Bible Dictionary defines contentment as "a state of mind in which one's desires are confined to his lot, whatever it may be."[53] This calm outlook accepts the situation at hand. There is no unease or angst. Serenity is based on the assurance God is in control, even if the current reality has difficulty. Events will unfold as they should. Even as Paul awaited his earthly fate, he had no doubts about his eternal destination.

On the way to Rome for trial, Paul endured 14 storm-driven days in the Adriatic Sea, then a shipwreck on Malta where a poisonous snake bit him. He knew suffering (Acts 27-28). However, he managed an incredible equanimity. What was his secret? "I can do all this through him who gives me strength" (Philippians 4:13). Jesus also equips you to handle whatever comes.

The going may be tough because of external circumstances, and you also may struggle with internal issues. Paul had a physical ailment he begged God to remove, but the answer was "No." Paul accepted his pain, saying God told him, "My grace is sufficient for you, for my

---

52 Editors of Encyclopedia Britannica, "Letter of Paul to the Philippians," Encyclopedia Britannica, August 18, 2020, https://www.britannica.com/topic/Letter-of-Paul-to-the-Philippians.

53 Bible Hub, "Contentment,." https://biblehub.com/topical/c/contentment.htm (accessed April 9, 2021).

power is made perfect in weakness" (2 Corinthians 12:9). No one likes to hurt, and bucking against daily pain takes enormous willpower.

Job is another person who understood trial. Even after he lost his fortune in livestock when marauders heisted his oxen, donkeys, and camels, he remained steadfast God would provide. Next, all his children died on a single day when a freak desert storm collapsed the house (Job 1:18-19). Despite these catastrophes, Job's faith was so strong when he heard the news, he fell to the ground in worship. He said, "Naked I came from my mother's womb, and naked I will depart. The Lord gave and the Lord has taken away; may the name of the Lord be praised" (Job 1:20-21).

Can you be as resolute facing misfortunes? Job hurt and wished for different outcomes. He cried out to God in pain and asked what in the world was going on. In suffering, he regretted the day he was born. "Do not mortals have hard service on earth?" he agonized (Job 7:1).

His life wasn't a cakewalk. He went from financial security to destitution, through no fault of his own. He endured grief and physical ailments. "My body is clothed with worms and scabs, my skin is broken and festering" (Job 7:5).

As he wrestled with God in the miserable nights how to make sense of the agony, the one thing Job didn't do was give up. He kept crying out to God for answers. He requested an audience to discuss what was going on. Job had an all-out commitment to God—even unto death. "Though he slay me, yet will I hope in him" (Job 13:15).

Both Job and Paul suffered intense physical pain and emotional loss, yet they refused to abandon God. These men knew the one place they could find peace was in his presence. They sought him, despite adversity, to bolster their understanding how to move forward. The faithful followers kept believing in God though the enemy threw every hardship their way to sabotage their confidence. Job and Paul kept faith, and you can too.

When your strength fails and you can't move another muscle, rest in the Lord's embrace like a little child in a loving parent's arms.

"But I have calmed and quieted myself; like a weaned child with its mother, like a weaned child I am content" (Psalm 131:2-3). An infant snuggles up closely and rests a chin on the parent's shoulder. Nothing else matters but the warmth of touch and gentle beating of the heart. Being together is enough.

When you have run the good race and ended up with a bruised heel and torn tendon, step back and rest. Regroup. Trust God to empower you to do whatever needs to be done tomorrow. But for now, cuddle up in that rocking chair and enjoy the evening. "O Israel, put your hope in the Lord both now and forevermore" (Psalm 131:3). Tomorrow dawns a new day.

God promises he will watch over your life; the Lord will watch over your coming and going both now and forevermore (Psalm 121:7-8).

FOR REFLECTION

"Though he slay me, yet will I hope in him" (Job 13:15).

What happens to your faith when calamity hits? Like Job and Paul, are you able to remember all the times God has secured you? Wait confidently to see how God will redeem in this circumstance too. If in the interim, you get discouraged and cry out in pain, God understands.

There is nothing wrong with an honest conversation with him. However, the mark of spiritual maturity is knowing even amid loss, you can find contentment. Look around and see the simple assurances of God's presence in the smile of a passerby or the expanse of the blue sky. He will bring you through this difficult season stronger and more resolute than ever.

A PRAYER FOR TODAY

Dear Lord, I love those moments of quiet with you when all is right in the world. I can find this whenever I set my mind on you. Help me take a mental break to feel your presence beside me. Thank you for always being available. Amen

Chapter Nineteen

GRACE IN THE STORM

Cold air blasts you like opening a walk-in freezer. Purple clouds bully the sky and threaten the horizon. Wind whips by your ears as tree tops writhe with nervous expectation. Forecasters predict a storm, and nature's early warning signs confirm it. Danger lies ahead, and you can smell its pungent approach.

News headlines broadcast chaos: three young stabbing victims found in an apartment; volcano eruption; nuclear terrorism; and assault-style weapons sales.[54] You wished you'd never looked. Pain radiates, and many wonder when God will intervene. As you look in the distance, you have a choice: cower in fear or brace yourself. While days full of sunshine delight, the tempests reveal God's might.

He is just, and there will be a reckoning for every evil act. "The Lord takes vengeance on his foes and vents his wrath against his enemies" (Nahum 1:2). Too often, societies have dismissed God as a fictional Santa in the sky who drops presents during holiday seasons for those who have been nice. Limiting the almighty God to such a caricature is a grievous error. He sees everything. He knows every secret. "For the eyes of the Lord are on the righteous and his ears are attentive to their prayer, but the face of the Lord is against those who do evil" (1 Peter 3:12).

---

54 National Public Radio, https://www.npr.org/sections/news/ (accessed April 11, 2021).

Perhaps you've been on the receiving end of dirty doings. Shoddy surgery cripples you. A client reneges on a contract and you face bankruptcy. One temperamental boss forces you to resign rather than wage a protracted legal defense you can't afford. A hacker steals your identity and ruins your credit. The list of horrors is long. Maybe you wonder why God has done nothing about the wrongs. The best mantra for you to repeat in the interim is "YET."

God tolerates no foolishness. His memory is long. While he will give a grace period and make allowances for people to change their ways, he has judgment for the wicked who are bent on destruction. The Lord of the millennia may seem slow to respond, but a century to him is a mere blink of the eye.

"But do not forget this one thing, dear friends: With the Lord a day is like a thousand years, and a thousand years are like a day. The Lord is not slow in keeping his promise, as some understand slowness. Instead, he is patient with you, not wanting anyone to perish, but everyone to come to repentance" (2 Peter 3:8-9).

God's scope of understanding ranges from the beginning of time to the end of the age. A study of history helps you see how he moves. Nineveh was the capital city of Assyria around 733 B.C., and near there is where God had the whale vomit Jonah to preach.[55] When Jonah complained about the assignment to correct foreigners about ungodly lifestyles, God chided, "And should I not have concern for the great city of Nineveh, in which there are more than a hundred and twenty thousand people who cannot tell their right hand from their left?" (Jonah 4:11).

Reluctantly, Jonah traveled to the metropolis to preach against wickedness, but his message resulted in hearts changing. Even the king of the Ninevites declared, "Let everyone call urgently on God. Let them give up their evil ways and their violence" (Jonah 3:8).

---

55 Chris and Jennifer Taylor, "Jonah Arrives at Nineveh," The Bible Journey, https://www.thebiblejourney.org/biblejourney2/41-jonah-goes-to-nineveh-and-nahum-condemns-it/jonah-arrives-at-nineveh/ (accessed April 11, 2021).

Because Jonah faithfully delivered warning and the people responded, God spared the city.

However, the Ninevites gradually forgot Jonah's instructions. For another 70 years, God monitored the Assyrians' decaying spiritual condition. When they became so decadent there was no desire for change, God again sent a messenger to warn about judgment. Around 663 B.C., a prophet from Judah named Nahum told the oppressing Assyrians God would hold them accountable for their cruelty.[56] Nineveh was a "city of blood, full of lies, and never without victims" (Nahum 3:1-4).

God's patience with the Assyrians ceased. "Nothing can heal you; your wound is fatal. All who hear the news about you clap their hands at your fall, for who has not felt your endless cruelty?" (Nahum 3:19). Finally, Babylonians ravaged Nineveh in 612 B.C.[57]

Because God cares about justice, he holds people accountable for their decisions. Woe to those who don't heed his commands, nor plead for his mercy. "Wail, for the day of the Lord is near; it will come like destruction from the Almighty. Because of this, all hands will go limp, every heart will melt with fear" (Isaiah 13:6-7).

Pity those who thought they could carry on as they pleased without consequence. "From the throne came flashes of lightning, rumblings, and peals of thunder" (Revelation 4:5). A category five hurricane, which has winds at or exceeding 157 miles per hour, causes catastrophic damage.[58] God's wrath at wrongdoers makes gale force winds look like a small puff. There will be no hiding or escaping God's investigation. His court is in session. Evidence is being compiled and witnesses aligned.

---

56 Chris and Jennifer Taylor, "Jonah Arrives at Nineveh," The Bible Journey, https://www.thebiblejourney.org/biblejourney2/41-jonah-goes-to-nineveh-and-nahum-condemns-it/jonah-arrives-at-nineveh/ (accessed April 11, 2021).

57 Ibid.

58 Abigail Abrams, "What Do Hurricane Categories Actually Mean?" *Time,* Updated August 28, 2019 https://time.com/4946730/hurricane-categories/#:~:text=In%20a%20Category%205%20hurricane,are%20157%20mph%20or%20higher (accessed April 14, 2021).

Even if people feel like they have successfully concealed their sins from others, God knows. Though human voices may be silenced, God's earthly creation witnesses events and testifies before the heavenly throne room about crimes committed. In Genesis, Cain kills his brother out of jealousy. Cain thinks he has hidden his offense and will get off scot-free. He deceived only himself.

"What have you done?" the Lord said. "Listen. Your brother's blood cries out to me from the ground. Now you are under a curse and driven from the ground, which opened its mouth to receive your brother's blood from your hand" (Genesis 4:10-11). Cain's evil act resulted in banishment from God's presence.

Christ is the defense counsel for those who follow God. Jesus is available to represent all, at his own personal cost. However, he only testifies to the judge on behalf of those defendants who accept him as their personal advocate. "My dear children, I write this to you so that you will not sin. But if anybody does sin, we have an advocate with the Father—Jesus Christ, the Righteous One. He is the atoning sacrifice for our sins, and not only for ours but also for the sins of the whole world" (1 John 2:1-2).

While Jesus is full of mercy, he isn't a pushover. He will fulfill the law. "Do not think that I have come to abolish the Law or the Prophets; I have not come to abolish them but to fulfill them," Jesus said. "For truly I tell you, until heaven and earth disappear, not the smallest letter, not the least stroke of a pen, will by any means disappear from the Law until everything is accomplished" (Matthew 5:17-18).

For a short period, perpetrators of crimes may seem to get off on technicalities. Juries may get hung and cases result in mistrials. A killer seems to evade capture. But God's justice is true and final. "For we must all appear before the judgment seat of Christ, so that each of us may receive what is due us for the things done while in the body, whether good or bad" (2 Corinthians 5:10).

God's holiness is a fearsome sight. His fury at the mistreatment of his beloved will know no bounds. Lightning bolts of indignation will sear gray skies, and mortar rounds of his outrage will explode, sending tremors throughout wrongdoers. "His way is in the whirlwind and the storm, and clouds are the dust of his feet" (Nahum 1:3). Heavy drops of righteousness will pummel the backs of the wicked as they try to hide in caves (Revelation 6:15). But there will be no escaping the final appearance before the heavenly throne.

John reported a vision of the end times while in exile on the island of Patmos. "Then I saw a great white throne and him who was seated on it. The earth and the heavens fled from his presence, and there was no place for them. And I saw the dead, great and small, standing before the throne, and books were opened....The dead were judged according to what they had done as recorded in the books" (Revelation 20:11-12).

When it is your turn to approach God's bench, what will you say? As a sinner, you have broken commands. Maybe you have turned away from Jesus at crucial times, even as Peter did the morning the roosters crowed.

"I don't know the man!" Peter cried, fearing discovery as a disciple when Jesus was undergoing trial (Matthew 26:74).

Have you distanced yourself from Jesus when a conversation about religion came up? Maybe you remained silent and failed to make a declaration of faith because of hecklers.

"Immediately, a rooster crowed. Then Peter remembered the word Jesus had spoken: 'Before the rooster crows, you will disown me three times' " (Matthew 26:74-75). After this denial, Peter went outside and sobbed at his weakness. Peter's fear outweighed his faith.

Think back to times in your life when you fell short. You tried to remain hidden in the shadows because stepping up to defend godly principles seemed too costly.

What are the charges against you? Satan is the prosecutor, and he will sidle up to the bench wearing wingtips of alligator hide. "Your Honor, this person is a menace to society. No clemency should be offered. This person needs to be locked up for life."

You shuffle forward in your orange jumpsuit. Your eyes can't meet the blazing fire of the judge who stares down at you, so you bow your head in shame. "Sir, I plead guilty," you utter softly.

Then another person's confident voice beside you rings out, "Your Honor, I ask this court to extend mercy." Jesus looks at you and smiles. "I can testify personally to the changed heart and rehabilitation that has occurred."

Silence pervades the courtroom as the robed judge raises the gavel. "I pronounce the defendant not guilty because of insufficient evidence from the prosecution."

The smirk on Satan's face disappears. Joy wells up in your heart as you realize you have been acquitted. The judge adds, "You are free to go."

Jesus grabs you in a bear hug, then claps you on the back. You look up to see loved ones surge toward you. As you turn to leave with them, another orange suit approaches the judge.

Only this time, Jesus ignores the defendant. When the judge looks toward Jesus, Jesus comments about the criminal on trial, "I never knew you. Away from me, you evildoers!" (Matthew 7:23). The bailiff marches that handcuffed convict out the back door.

The final verdict is God's. Though his wheels of justice may roll more slowly than you'd like, he will acquit the righteous and sentence the guilty. There will be a reckoning for all.

God promises he is slow to anger and great in power, but he will not leave the guilty unpunished (Nahum 1:3).

FOR REFLECTION

"The Lord, the Lord, the compassionate and gracious God, slow to anger, abounding in love and faithfulness, maintaining love to thousands, and forgiving wickedness, rebellion and sin. Yet he does not leave the guilty unpunished" (Exodus 34:6-7).

"Seek the Lord while he may be found; call on him while he is near. Let the wicked forsake their ways and the unrighteous their thoughts. Let them turn to the Lord, and he will have mercy on them, and to our God, for he will freely pardon" (Isaiah 55:6-7).

You may have been a victim of others' cruelty. Can you trust God to resolve those wrongs in his own time and way? There will be an accounting.

Meanwhile, are you able to be honest with yourself for bad things *you've* done? Imagine Jesus as your attorney. His defense will not be built on your works, but on his personal sacrifice made of love. Thank him for all he does for you.

A PRAYER FOR TODAY

Dear Lord, I trust you to right the wrongs done to me. I will not act out of vengeance, but instead rely on you to hold others accountable for their actions. Please give me the ability to pray for my enemies and allow you to enforce justice in your timing and your way. Amen

Chapter Twenty

SURPRISING
OUTCOMES

$\mathcal{P}$lans go awry. Despite careful organization and methodical implementation, you can't control outcomes. God does, and sometimes he interrupts a routine to showcase the divine. His ways are higher than those of humans. Consider the difference between a teen flying a remote-controlled hobby plane and a seasoned veteran in the cockpit of a Boeing 747 full of passengers. Both people enjoy flight, but there is no comparison in skill and experience.

The same can be said for you and God. He is in the heavenly control tower monitoring worldwide flight patterns. Our heavenly Father tracks weather around the globe for emerging concerns. He computes speeds, times, and distances and communicates with clear instructions for pilots in all languages. God coordinates multiple flights simultaneously and prioritizes needs. The Lord concentrates in a place where many conversations occur at once and never misses a radio call.

If he reroutes your flight plan, who are you to argue?

For 2019, the Federal Aviation Administration's Air Traffic Organization tabulated more than 45,000 flights in 2.9 million square miles of airspace.[59] How much more does God juggle in his kingdom? He has myriad angels, not to mention humans throughout eons.

---

59 Federal Aviation Administration's Air Traffic Organization, "Air Traffic by the Numbers," https://www.faa.gov/air_traffic/by_the_numbers/ (accessed April 16, 2021).

Jesus said, "Do you think I cannot call on my Father, and he will at once put at my disposal more than twelve legions of angels?" (Matthew 26:53). One researcher estimated a Roman legion would have 6,000 cavalrymen, plus support staff.[60] That means Jesus could muster more than 72,000 angels in one moment! These fearsome creatures aren't at all like the cutesy cherubs in lawn ornaments or Valentine's Day greeting cards. God's angels will be tasked with throwing evil beings into the blazing furnace when Jesus cleans his kingdom (Matthew 13:40-42).

The thing is, humans resist what they don't understand. People want to contain life in clearly labeled boxes, and they get anxious when things don't fit nicely. God likes to reveal himself in new ways to those adventurers who allow him the opportunity. He is always up to something for a higher purpose.

The book of Judges tells the story of a woman, married to Manoah of Zorah, who could not have children. At home one day, she had the unexpected happen. Maybe she was hanging out clothes to dry or sweeping the courtyard, but the mundane got interrupted when a stranger stopped by to give her startling news. "You are barren and childless, but you are going to become pregnant and give birth to a son" (Judges 13:3).

The lady may have had her mouth hang open in shock. Who wouldn't if a man you didn't know blurted out your most private concerns, then said you would have a baby? The angel of the Lord added, "Now see to it that you drink no wine or other fermented drink and that you do not eat anything unclean. You will become pregnant and have a son" (Judges 13:4-5).

While the woman was delighted to hear she would have an infant to put in the heirloom crib, the child's arrival had a larger purpose than blessing her and her husband. The angel's further instructions included no razor may be used on the child's hair because "The boy is to be a

---

60 N. S. Gill, "The Varied Size of the Roman Legions," Thought Co., September 23, 2018, https://www.thoughtco.com/the-size-of-the-roman-legions-120873 (accessed April 16, 2021).

Nazirite, dedicated to God from the womb. He will take the lead in delivering Israel from the hands of the Philistines" (Judges 13:5).

The woman ran to share the news with her husband. "A man of God came to me. He looked like an angel of God, very awesome. I didn't ask him where he came from, and he didn't tell me his name" (Judges 13:6).

The second half of that quote is good for a giggle. Angels appearing could rattle anyone. Who would have the composure to politely inquire, "Sorry, sir, I didn't catch your name. And where exactly are you from?"

Her husband believed what she relayed, and he prayed to the Lord for another visitation so the couple could get guidance how to raise this special son. Though Manoah prayed, the angel appeared to the wife a second time while she was in the field alone. She probably pinched herself to make sure she wasn't dreaming. Then she hustled to find her hubby. "He's here! The man who appeared to me the other day!" (Judges 13:10).

Manoah came out to meet the man and confirmed the exciting news. When Manoah invited the newcomer to stay for dinner, he declined and suggested preparing the meal as a burnt offering to the Lord instead. Manoah also asked the man for his name. By this time, the angel felt a bit testy. "Why do you ask my name? It is beyond understanding" (Judges 13:18).

Manoah must have had doubts, even as he desperately hoped the prophecy would come true. To alleviate any uncertainty Manoah may have had, God amazed the couple by having the messenger ascend the flames of the blazing offering on the altar. The pair fell on their faces at this development. The man feared their demise, but his wife calmed him saying, "If the Lord had meant to kill us, he would not have accepted a burnt offering and grain offering from our hands, nor shown us all these things or now told us this" (Judges 13:22-23).

Months later, the woman gave birth to a son named Samson, who matured with incredible strength to wreak havoc on the Philistines, as long as he kept his mane long.

Another surprising twist God wrote into his history involves a talking donkey. Yes, you read that right. An ordinary pack animal with big floppy ears received the ability to communicate with a rider going the wrong way. In the ancient Near East, Balaam was known as one who could wield great political power. People in the area sought him for insights what to do because they recognized him as a seer. Picture him with a paunch from a life of privilege and black robes that befitted the solemnity of his station as messenger of the gods.

Per the custom of that time, kings would seek oracles to determine the course of battle prior to engaging in combat.[61] In particular, a Moabite king wanted to get help to drive out the Israelites settling in the area from Egypt. The Moabites feared the large numbers of Israelites would take over everything (Numbers 22:1-11).

Balaam was happy to receive the Moabites' payment for divination and inquired of God for them. He probably combed his long black beard with satisfaction about the opportunity. However, God told Balaam the Moabites would not be victorious because he favored the Israelites. "You must not put a curse on those people, because they are blessed" (Numbers 22:12). Balaam repeated God's message, then told the Moabite princes to go back to their country.

But the king of Moab sent another more distinguished group of ambassadors who promised a truly handsome compensation if only Balaam cursed the new arrivals. Caving in to the Moabite pressure, Balaam saddled his donkey the next morning and went with the Moabite escort. God wasn't pleased. Perhaps Balaam's greed got the better of him or perhaps he enjoyed the royal attention insinuating he as a mere man could determine the fate of armies. God let Balaam

---

61 Jo Ann Hackett, "The Story of Balaam," Bible Odyssey, https://www.bibleodyssey.org/en/places/related-articles/the-story-of-balaam (accessed April 18, 2021).

ride that donkey, but he didn't let him parade far with the distinguished retinue.

Angry that Balaam consorted with the enemy, God sent an angel to intercept him. Balaam's mount saw the angel blocking the path ahead and balked, digging in its hooves and refusing to go forward. Apparently, Balaam was so busy picturing coffers of coins, he missed seeing the angel guard's drawn sword. The donkey didn't and veered off to a field.

Clueless, Balaam beat the skittish donkey until it moved forward. Ahead lay a narrow walled path between two vineyards. The donkey again saw the angel and shied against the rocky border, crushing Balaam's foot. So he whipped it again.

Have you been blind to warnings the same way as Balaam and taken out your frustration on an innocent party? If your way forward is blocked repeatedly, it would be wise to stop and inquire of the Lord.

A third time the angel moved into a position preventing the animal from proceeding. This time, the mount lay down. Enraged, Balaam beat it with his staff. How embarrassing for him not to control a simple burro when the Moabite princes expected he could turn the tide of a military campaign. Nearby soldiers must have snickered under their breath at his incompetence.

Then God used the voice of a "dumb" animal to shake up Balaam's sense of self importance. The donkey asked its owner in a husky voice, "What have I done to you to make you beat me these three times?" (Numbers 13:28). Picture here its sad brown eyes and a quivering muzzle.

Hearing an animal speak doesn't seem to faze Balaam's rage. He doesn't apologize or hug its fuzzy neck. His belligerence is in full blast. "You have made a fool of me! If only I had a sword in my hand, I would kill you right now" (Numbers 22:29). Did the Moabites hear this exchange? Or did they only hear Balaam's side of the conversation? Maybe the Moabites raised their eyebrows and motioned circles around their temples indicating Balaam must be crazy.

The donkey didn't start braying. It rose on little black hooves and reasoned, "Am I not your own donkey, which you have always ridden, to this day? Have I been in the habit of doing this to you?" (Numbers 22:30).

Who are the people who speak truth to you when you are on a tear and going down the wrong path? Do you berate them in your head-strong pursuit? Think about whom God has placed to give you solid advice, even though you may not accord that person "equal" status.

As soon as Balaam acknowledged the donkey's usual obedience, God opened Balaam's eyes to see the armed angel, who immediately fussed at Balaam for beating the donkey. "I have come here to oppose you because your path is reckless before me. The donkey saw me and turned away from me these three times. If it had not turned away, I would certainly have killed you by now, but I would have spared it" (Numbers 22:33).

Sometimes God allows quiet, hard-working people to see what the spiritually "elite" miss because they are too full of themselves. Be careful basking in delivering God's messages because there is a real risk you can become blind to God's mission. With any attempt to contact God for insider tidbits, be sure to check your heart first. If the motive is personal gain or prestige, you are in a place where correction will occur.

Balaam apologized for his presumption and acknowledged his sin. God directed him to go with the Moabites and speak only what he was told. Balaam served as a faithful oracle then and steadfastly blessed the Israelites, despite the Moabites' ire. He learned the Giver of insights wasn't to be manipulated for profit.

Undeterred, the Moabites staged several increasingly elaborate pageants with sacrifices. But when Balaam asked God what to say each time, the answer to the Moabites was to forget attacking the Israelites. Instead of the Moabites bestowing honors on Balaam, they wanted to curse him for failing to send them off with reassurances.

Balaam's visions of grandeur evaporated when the Moabite king ousted him from the country and refused to pay any compensation.

"Now leave at once and go home!" the Moabite king roared. "I said I would reward you handsomely, but the Lord has kept you from being rewarded" (Numbers 24:11).

The Moabites gave up orchestrating a curse to undermine God's favored people. God will not be thwarted. He alone will control the destiny of all. His ways are higher.

> **God promises as the heavens are higher than the earth, so are his ways higher than those of humans (Isaiah 55:8-9).**

FOR REFLECTION

"I have come here to oppose you because your path is a reckless one before me. The donkey saw me and turned away from me these three times. If it had not turned away, I would certainly have killed you by now, but I would have spared it" (Judges 22:33).

Have you, or someone you know, experienced a visitation from a heavenly messenger? What were the circumstances and how did you or the person react? How did that experience enlighten you about God's care?

Perhaps an animal has shielded you from harm. Somehow, that creature knew a danger existed of which you were unaware. Have you been protected during a reckless pursuit? One way to test for legitimacy of counsel is if the messenger gives glory only to God. If the person seeks recognition for himself or herself, beware.

A PRAYER FOR TODAY

*Dear Lord, I don't understand many of your ways. I look at the
height of the galaxies and depth of the oceans and feel small. Your
power overwhelms me. Please help me be like the wife of Manoah
and believe in miraculous messages that bring hope and life. Please
protect me from Balaam's stubborn rebellion that caused
a donkey's intervention. Amen*

Chapter Twenty-One

JESUS IS TITANIUM

Superman had green radioactive kryptonite. Snow White had the luscious red poisoned apple. Achilles had the unprotected heel after being dipped in the river Styx. These fictional characters had a key weakness that threatened to ruin them. While Superman, Snow White, and Achilles acted in imaginations, Jesus suffered in reality. His vulnerability was the cross.

However, what appeared to human eyes to be Jesus' undoing actually catapulted him forward into victory. Occasionally, you turn situations upside down to make them right. "For Christ also suffered once for sins, the righteous for the unrighteous, to bring you to God" (1 Peter 3:18). Though Jesus committed no crime, he stood in for all whom God will judge for their wrongdoings. Jesus took on the blame and satisfied the penalty so you could go free.

Crucifixion—a horrible, slow way to die—served as capital punishment to warn others not to buck the establishment. First, there was the public humiliation of being hoisted on a wooden beam, naked, in front of everyone with the crime posted on a sign above the head. Passersby stared at the convicted, watching the poor souls gasp for air as their lungs strained for oxygen and organs failed as circulation constricted.[62] The execution could take hours, and as each minute passed,

62 Editors of Encyclopedia Britannica. "Crucifixion," https://www.britannica.com/topic/crucifixion-capital-punishment, (accessed April 18, 2021).

the agony grew. Of the world religions, Jesus is the *only* deity to stand in for his people and pay the price for their eternal redemption.

Satan watched Jesus' suffering from the sidelines and gloated about the pending defeat, but Satan seriously underestimated his opponent. Imagine here the "My Turn" battle scene from the 2008 Iron Man movie. Tony Stark is taken captive, but he emerges from the cave of his imprisonment more powerful than ever.[63] Jesus also had strength Satan hadn't conceived. Similar to how water has three forms—solid, liquid, and vapor—Jesus shed physical constraints to transcend dimensions as the prince of heaven.

Rather than collapsing under Satan's pressure, Jesus forged a new covenant. "He who descended is the very one who ascended higher than all the heavens, in order to fill the whole universe" (Ephesians 4:10). Before Satan could swipe the sneer off his face, Jesus had dominion of not only heaven and earth, but Hades too. With new authority, Jesus wasted no time raiding darkness to bring light.

Jesus plundered Satan's stronghold to free hostages. "He (Jesus) was put to death in the body but made alive in the Spirit. After being made alive, he went and made proclamation to the imprisoned spirits—to those who were disobedient long ago when God waited patiently in the days of Noah while the ark was being built" (1 Peter 3:18-20). You can infer from this passage those who had disobeyed centuries before now heard Jesus' good news—in person!

The ark saved only eight people at the time. However, the new baptism is the resurrection of Jesus Christ "who has gone into heaven and is at God's right hand—with angels, authorities, and powers in submission to him" (1 Peter 3:22).

Jesus is titanium. He is strong, flexible, and corrosion resistant.[64] Discovery of his new mettle floored demonic adversaries. The moment Jesus surrendered his earthly life, the earth shook, rocks split, and tombs

---

63 "Iron Man (2008) – My Turn Scene (4/9) Movieclips," YouTube, https://www.youtube.com/watch?v=GH-r4HXHcCk, (accessed April 18, 2021).

64 "Titanium," Nippon Steel, August 4, 2017, https://www.nipponsteel.com/en/product/titan/feature/.

opened. "Bodies of many holy people who had died were raised to life" (Matthew 27:52). Nothing could hold back Jesus' power.

With his face shining like the sun in all its brilliance, Jesus says to you: "Do not be afraid. I am the First and the Last. I am the Living One; I was dead, and now look, I am alive for ever and ever!" (Revelation 1:17-18).

Nothing can stop the love of Christ for you. He will storm every garrison and open sealed crypts to free you. Death doesn't faze him. He's already been there, done that. His willing sacrifice netted him extraordinary control. "I hold the keys of death and Hades" (Revelation 1:18). Keys symbolize ownership, and no place is off limits to Jesus.

Precisely because Jesus walked in the dank dungeon of death and smelled rotten despair, he makes it his mission to rescue the captives. If you ever have been in jail or visited a prison, you understand the barrenness of gray block walls and the ominous metal clanging as double doors slam and lock behind you. As you go deeper into the bowels of the facility, there are no windows and the air is stale. There are no pictures of smiling faces nor homey touches of colorful rugs. The atmosphere is bleak and so are the faces. Time creeps by in staccato seconds.

As you lie on your thin mattress and stare at the grungy wall, you hear the jangle of keys. You roll over, expecting the jailer, only to see that Jesus comes to claim your imprisoned soul. "You see, at just the right time, when we were still powerless, Christ died for the ungodly" (Romans 5:6). Jesus pays a visit to your barred cell and uses unconditional love to unlock the door. He frees you and invites you to join him ascending to God's throne.

"God demonstrates his own love for us in this: while we were still sinners, Christ died for us" (Romans 5:8). Crime is bloody and damages lives. God will not allow sin to go unpunished. However, God accepts restitution made on your behalf by Jesus so justice prevails.

"Christ is the mediator of a new covenant, that those who are called may receive the promised eternal inheritance—now that he has died as a ransom to set them free from the sins committed under the first covenant" (Hebrews 9:15). Christ has no illusions about the filthy ways of mankind. He has seen the worst, but he also forgives and empowers you to move forward into new life, if you seek him.

He will usher you from the claustrophobic cells of shame and defeat into sunlit expanses where you can draw in deep lungfuls of fresh air. He proceeds like a victor of old in a triumphant parade toward the Father. "Sing to God, sing in praise of his name, extol him who rides on the clouds; rejoice before him—his name is the Lord" (Psalm 68:4). Jesus, as God's emissary on earth, leads forth the prisoners with singing (Psalm 68:6).

When Jesus ascends to celebrate victory, he leads beloved captives in his train (Psalm 68:18). Today's homecoming parades, similar to the triumphal returning marches of ancient generals, showcase the best of a community. So does Jesus enter his Father's throne room with the company of saved souls in tow. "The chariots of God are tens of thousands and thousands of thousands; the Lord has come from Sinai into his sanctuary" (Psalm 68:17). Jesus bows to his Father, then presents the eager crowd he has redeemed.

Picture the joy on the Father's face as he beholds his children restored to him. Seated high and exalted on his throne, he extends the scepter of favor toward his son. As God stands and walks to embrace each person, the train of his pure white robe sparkles with the precious jewels that are his ransomed who have returned.

The voices of these redeemed shout in joy. "Praise be to the Lord, to God our Savior, who daily bears our burdens. Our God is a God who saves; from the Sovereign Lord comes escape from death" (Psalm 68:19-20). You can be sure Jesus will come to save you. He storms the doors of death to take back his own, and he is not limited by a physical dimension nor historical era.

His timetable is eternal, and he wants you with him. "Neither death nor life, neither angels nor demons, neither the present nor the future, nor any powers, neither height nor depth, nor anything else in all creation, will be able to separate us from the love of God that is in Christ Jesus our Lord" (Romans 8:37-39).

The cross wasn't the end. That instrument of suffering was instead a gateway that unlocked a heavenly future for you. So if you struggle now, hold on. Jesus is on his way to you. "But if we hope for what we do not yet have, we wait for it patiently" (Romans 8:25).

> ### God promises Jesus is with you always, to the very end of the age (Matthew 28:20).

FOR REFLECTION

"You will keep in perfect peace those whose minds are steadfast, because they trust in you. Trust in the Lord forever, for the Lord, the Lord himself, is the Rock eternal" (Isaiah 26:3).

What is dead in your life? Your career? Your dreams? Jesus set aside his sovereignty to suffer on a cross. That seems an odd way to achieve victory.

What trial are you willing to endure to show how much you love? Take heart that even in the darkest moments when all options seem to have expired, God will raise up solutions beyond any you could imagine.

Reflect on dead-ends you've experienced. How has time revealed those disappointments as gateways to greater truths? Pray for God to give you eyes to see hope and open doors. Commit to interceding for others who feel trapped so they might find resurrection.

A PRAYER FOR TODAY

Dear Lord, The pain of Jesus' crucifixion scares me. His awful death makes me sad. Yet only his willing sacrifice defeated the enemy and made it possible for me to approach your throne as a beloved child. I want to serve you, not myself, but my ego keeps getting in the way. Focus my eyes on my savior and doing only what he would ask of me this day. Amen

Chapter Twenty-Two

FAMILY REUNION

*F*ather waits at the mountain top under the shade of huge cedars and watches for you. The lawn chair creaks as he shifts his weight, craning his neck for a better view of the winding driveway leading up to the homestead. A well-tended lawn fans out from the magnificent stone mansion that has been the family seat for generations. Father smokes a pipe with chocolate-flavored tobacco as he scans the horizon for dust clouds signaling the approach of your car.

He can't wait for your arrival. He has missed you so much. Homecoming is going to be awesome. Family from every corner of the world will gather. Father has made all the arrangements. Michael will run airport shuttles to chauffeur travelers from remote regions such as Scotland, Antarctica, and Australia.

Others emerge from packed vehicles and crowd the driveway. Car doors slam and excited conversations carry in the breeze as loved ones congregate. Father circulates, greeting each person with a warm smile and hug. You'll hear excited chatter as relatives catch up on news. "Hey, Billy, looking good," a man shouts over the melee to another with unruly black hair. A slender teen offers his arm to an elderly woman in a pink cardigan as she moves toward the front door. Laughter rings out as children play chase and run around the stately trees while adults look on good-naturedly.

Grandparents embrace youth as siblings high five. Being together again feels good. Delicious aromas waft from the open kitchen window. Father has prepared a feast to celebrate everyone being home. Blackberry cobblers and cherry pies cool on the sill, while the mouth-watering aroma of hickory smoke from the grill draws onlookers toward the cobblestone patio arranged with geraniums in clay pots.

Father has been planning this get-together for a long time and has spared no expense setting up the party. Giant harps broadcast soothing music along cords running overhead like almost-invisible awnings. Imagine the outdoor concerts of William Close's Earth Harp with 1,000-foot-long strings. [65][66] The air vibrates with ever-unfolding improvisation from musicians creating joyous sounds.

Father is delighted with the relatives assembled. Dark-skinned Ethiopians chat with freckled Spaniards. Long-bearded Jews toss bean bags and play corn hole with Chinese businessmen attired in button-down shirts with rolled-up sleeves. Ladies in bright saris and delicate gold bangles sit in wicker chairs on the covered porch and visit with women wearing medieval bodices and full skirts.

Before Father is a great multitude no one can count, from every nation, tribe, people, and language (Revelation 7:9). His family is home, where he's always longed for them to be—with him. As his gaze travels lovingly over each precious face, he sees children, grandchildren, great-grandchildren and more who testify to the faithfulness of his care.

"From everlasting to everlasting the Lord's love is with those who fear him, and his righteousness with their children's children—with those who keep his covenant and remember to obey his precepts" (Psalm 103:17-18). He knows the struggles each faced on the journey

---

65 Nadja Sayej, "The Earth Harp Is the Biggest Harp in the World," Noisey Music by Vice, December 16, 2013 https://www.vice.com/en/article/64bnj6/the-earth-harp-is-the-biggest-harp-in-the-world, (accessed April 24, 2021).

66 William Close, "The Earth Harp Collective Reel of Shows," YouTube, August 9, 2017 https://www.youtube.com/watch?v=qrjcOpq_Nw0, (accessed April 25, 2021).

of faith. Though individuals hail from different eras and geography, the question of the heart he asked each was the same: "Do you love me?"

"Yes" shout young adults who line up by the white sand volleyball court. They call Father over to referee a friendly match. He blows the whistle as he motions for the serve. A lanky 20-year-old tips the ball to a muscular girl. She expertly sets it for a stocky man with shoulder-length dreadlocks to spike it over the net. "Point." Applause breaks out.

Attracted to the commotion, a stately tiger saunters toward the sidelines. Luxurious fur ripples over taut muscles as its amber eyes rove. The large cat wears a diamond collar and chuffs a greeting to a delicate gazelle with a black stripe along its belly and a garland of fragrant flowers around its neck. The pair lays down in the shade, side by side (Isaiah 11:6-9). An armadillo scoots by with a mischievous boy in hot pursuit.

Mary, in a flowered dress with a yellow hibiscus behind her ear, approaches Father asking, "Where is Jesus? I can't find him anywhere." Disappointment laces her voice.

"Don't worry. He is on the way," Father answered. "He had one more person who needed a way to get here."

Sure enough, a few moments later, a VIP edition of a pure white Rolls Royce Phantom limousine parks right by the front door. A simple wooden cross the size of a man's hand decorates the hood. Before the uniformed driver can get out, the back passenger door swings open. Jesus emerges in black jeans and a T-shirt with the slogan "Real Men Love God." He stands to the side to make room for another person to get out. This one is in grungy clothes and torn shoes.

Father makes his way toward the pair, but before he can get close, the disheveled person mumbles, "Sir, I am unworthy to be a guest here" (Luke 15:21).

Unfazed, Father says to a nearby relative, "Quick. Bring the best robe and put it on him. Put a ring on his finger and sandals on his feet. For this son of mine was dead and is alive again; he was lost and is found" (Luke 15:22-24). Jesus gives a wave of support as the other man is surrounded by family and escorted inside the house.

Jesus steps forward to hug his father and says quietly, "I protected the family you entrusted to me and kept them safe" (John 17:12).

Father turns slightly toward members milling around the home. He rests his right arm along Jesus' broad shoulder and says, "You are my son whom I love. With you, I am well pleased" (Matthew 3:17, Mark 9:7, and 2 Peter 1:17).

A chubby red-head child of eight years skips up. "Let's play." As Jesus opens his palm to reach for the child, you see a sunken scar in the center. Jesus leans down, swings the child up over his head and onto his shoulders. Holding the little one's ankles securely, Jesus winks at Father, then gallops off making horse sounds.

Ꮚ Ꮚ Ꮚ Ꮚ Ꮚ

Later that night after the feasting, everyone gathers in the family room to watch old movies. Father sets up a high-definition screen and organizes reels while older relatives settle on comfy couches. Kids pile up on beanbags. Everyone is clean and wearing fleecy white bathrobes monogrammed with the infinity symbol. The smallest ones have on footie pajamas and cuddle next to parents.

The projector clicks as the movie begins. The dark screen shows a velvet black backdrop with pinpricks of light, then bright red and orange flares explode. What the world might call the "Big Bang" is Father's pyrotechnics. Fireworks of white light, purple pops and green streaks color the sky. "And God said, 'Let there be light'" intones the movie narrator (Genesis 1:3). While viewers in the family room "ooh" and "ahh" about beautiful constellations, the lens zeroes in on Saturn where Jesus glides on a ring like a playground slide. Everyone in the room watching chuckles, nudging each other. "There he goes again," they say. Jesus smiles.

In the show's next segment, viewers see a huge gray shape almost 100 feet long moving underwater in a periwinkle expanse. Strange low-frequency pulses fill the speakers. Lights dance upon the back of a blue whale as it sails along the sea (Psalm 104:26). When the gigantic creature breaks the surface to breathe, a huge spout of water bubbles up. On the top of the spray, Jesus bounces in flamingo swim trunks. "I wanna do that," a boy on the beanbag declares.

The storyboard takes a somber turn with the next image. A blaze of light erupts in the sky as the nuclear bomb detonates over Hiroshima in 1945. The narrator says, "Dust and debris from the destruction nearly blotted out the morning sun."[67] A camera pans to reveal a mushroom cloud of fire rising. In the foreground, a silhouette of Jesus cradles a crumpled body. Total silence fills the family room. In the next frame, Jesus lifts twisted wreckage to free a soul trapped below. Sorrow etches his face. The narrator's voice can be heard again: "My comfort in suffering is this: Your promise preserves my life" (Psalm 119:50).

Watchers in the home theater remember their times of trial and pain. They reach for the hand of the one next to them and squeeze with a gentle reassurance that all sorrow is behind them. They are home and safe now. There is no more pain. With Father, they are secure.

From the speakers, a musical score begins softly and gains volume. The cinema focuses upon a vast choir lined up in a pillared temple with dazzling light. Baritones to sopranos blend voices to sing:

"Where can I go from your Spirit?
Where can I flee from your presence?
If I go up to the heavens, you are there;
if I make my bed in the depths, you are there.
If I rise on the wings of the dawn, if I settle on the far side of the sea,
even there your right hand will guide me,
your right hand will hold me fast."

---

67 Evan Andrews, "The Man Who Survived Two Atomic Bombs," History, August 30, 2018, https://www.history.com/news/the-man-who-survived-two-atomic-bombs, (accessed April 24, 2021.

(Psalm 139:7-10)

Father clears his throat to get everyone's attention as the song trails off and the credits roll. In a deep voice, he says, "You are my beloved. There is nothing I won't do for you. For me, nothing is impossible."

He points to stone above the fireplace mantel engraved with the family motto:

"Love each other as I have loved you" (John 15:12).

God promises he will bring you home (Zephaniah 3:20).

FOR REFLECTION

"How great are his signs, how mighty his wonders! His kingdom is an eternal kingdom; his dominion endures from generation to generation" (Daniel 4:3).

Family reunions are times to celebrate being together. Separations make the reconnections all the sweeter. Whom do you miss and can't wait to see again?

How is God's family much larger than one denomination or bloodline? As you speak with people this week, imagine seeing them at the heavenly party. Might you treat them differently today if you know you will see them then?

A PRAYER FOR TODAY

Dear Lord, Being home with you is the greatest joy imaginable. Nothing can separate me from your love. Amen

ACKNOWLEDGMENTS

Thank you, God, for allowing me to travel this creative journey with much help.

Thank you to the first readers who were incredibly supportive:

Honey Smoak, Craig and Debbie Miley, Jackie Howe, Virgil and Pat Clark, Brenda Wickard, Letha Jones, George and Joan Firehammer, Betsy Johnson, Rhonda Smith, Lori Shire, Libby Wharton, Linda Connor, Kristin Willis, Michael L. Anderson, Harold Nelson, Meg Infiorati, and Lynn Copeland Buckles.

The pastoral support and prayers of Doug Kokx, Dawn Carter, and Anthony "Mac" Maccagnano of Living Hope Church proved indispensable. Thank you also to Keith Boyette and Steve Hay for shepherding me through many storms.

Much appreciation is expressed to Kathy Ide and Rhonda Rhea for their patient mentoring in the publication world. Word Weavers International and its Leesburg and Orlando Chapter critique groups offered tremendous insights on revisions. Bold Vision Books and the Porters supported me as a new author and made a huge investment to share this message.

Special acknowledgment goes to Ryan Sutherland for NIV updates.

Gratitude goes to Zondervan for the New International Version Scriptures and the Blue Letter Bible's free online search tool that made finding Bible verses so much easier.

MEET THE AUTHOR

A native Floridian, **Tracy L. Smoak** grew up riding horses and climbing citrus trees. Her passion is to encourage others in their faith journey. Smoak contributes to *Guideposts* and authored the contemporary fiction *Who Brought the Dog to Church?*. She loves photography and wrote three hardcover devotionals with her original color pictures (*Living Water to Refresh Your Soul* and *Arranged with Love*).

Smoak holds a master's in Education and a bachelor's in communication. At her church home, she leads small-group Bible studies. She is an active member of Word Weavers International. Her website is www.tracysmoak.com. Devotions with her photography set to music are available on YouTube at https://www.youtube.com/@tracysmoak/playlists.

.

Made in the USA
Columbia, SC
10 October 2023

23978130R00096